New Buildings in the Commonwealth

Startling changes in long established topographical patterns are taking
place in all quarters of the world as the tropical areas of the British
Commonwealth – hitherto largely undeveloped – emerge into nationhood, sophistication and the first stages of industrialization. Above is
Hong Kong, looking across the island city – where buildings on an un-
precedented scale can be seen rising among the old – to the harbour
beyond.

Edited by J. M. RICHARDS

NEW BUILDINGS IN THE COMMONWEALTH

THE ARCHITECTURAL PRESS LONDON

Foreword

A SHORT WHILE AGO *The Architectural Review*, aware that the building going forward in the various parts of the British Commonwealth was being given less attention than it deserved, decided to devote a couple of whole numbers to putting this right. These two numbers were published at the end of 1959 and in the middle of 1960. The considerable interest they aroused is the justification – if justification be needed – for reprinting the material contained in them in book form, together with some additional material that has since become available.

The first of *The Architectural Review's* special numbers dealt with the four large Dominions – Canada, South Africa, Australia and New Zealand – which for the most part lie in the temperate zones. It provides the first half of this book, except that the South African section has been omitted, South Africa having left the Commonwealth since the number was published. The second number, providing the rest of the book, dealt with the remaining Commonwealth territories which lie, in a general climatic sense if not wholly so in a strictly geographical sense, within the tropics. The material for the two numbers was collected with the help of numerous architects and others in each territory (who are thanked below) and, in the case of the number dealing with the Dominions, with the special help of my colleague, Professor Pevsner, who had recently visited each of them in turn. Professor Pevsner also played a large part in editing this number, which was otherwise my responsibility in my capacity as executive editor of *The Architectural Review*. It was similarly my responsibility to edit the second number, and it seemed reasonable for me to complete the task by editing the book which now emerges from the two numbers.

It has also been, I should add, a task of interest and pleasure. The countries dealt with in the two parts of the book are all rapidly developing, looking actively towards the future and, although varying greatly in scale, sophistication and resources, all full of architectural vitality. Their best buildings, therefore, are to be looked at not only for their intrinsic value but as an earnest of even more notable architecture to come.

The buildings illustrated herewith have been chosen to give a picture, as far as the space available allowed, of the most interesting architectural work done in each territory of the Commonwealth in the last few years. The original division into two parts – the large Dominions and the tropical territories – has been maintained because conditions in each are so different. The Dominions, by and large, share the same technical standards, the same degree of industrial development and architectural sophistication, as Europe and America. Theirs is an old civilization translated to wider spaces, rather than a new one based on differences of race and climate and culture. Buildings in the Dominions are designed, as in any European country, by local architects for the most part locally trained.

In the case of the tropical territories the position is altogether different, apart from the obvious fact that their buildings cater for very different climates. They are among the less developed areas of the world; they are inhabited for the most part by colonial or ex-colonial peoples vigorously emerging into nationhood and faced, while they do so, with the problem of assimilating European techniques and ideas of progress. Although, in due course, each territory will no doubt become self-sufficient architecturally, for most of them this will be a long process, and they are only now beginning to acquire their own architectural professions and architectural schools. Not till they have done so, perhaps, can they expect to achieve a consistent architectural style recognizably their own.

Most of the buildings from the tropical territories illustrated here were either designed in England by English architects (as in the case of many of those in West Africa), or they were designed by architects of British origin, largely trained in Britain or America, who practise locally. Often such practices are newly established, and architects are still feeling their way towards methods of work that suit the peculiarities of the place; but in several places, such as Hong Kong and Singapore, large buildings in a wholly western style have been dominating the skyline for several generations, and the newer, more modern, architecture there is the work of the successors of the Western-trained architects who designed them. In these cities, however, there now also flourish firms of Chinese and other native architects, and, before long, no doubt native African architects will be putting up important buildings in East and West Africa, and West Indian architects in the Caribbean. India is an example, from among the countries represented here, of one in which every building illustrated (except for the rather specialized case of Chandigarh and of Le Corbusier's work elsewhere) is the work of Indian architects.

The progress towards architectural self-sufficiency is one of the subjects touched upon in the short essays that introduce the various sections of the tropical half of this book. They also touch on such matters as climatic and social conditions and the availability of materials and skilled labour. Some knowledge of these is required for the purpose of understanding which qualities of the architecture shown arise from internal causes, and which from outside influences, and why the architecture of the various territories has much in common, but many points of difference.

I am grateful to the authors* of all the introductory essays – who are, for the most part, architects working in the territory they write about, or who have had experience of building there – for permission to reprint them. I have

---

* Among these authors was Professor Fred Laserre, whose tragic death in a climbing accident has since shocked his friends and colleagues. He wrote the article on Canada.

already referred to this book's indebtedness to Professor Pevsner, who contributes the introductory essay to the New Zealand section as well as a general introduction to the first part of the book dealing with the Dominions. The equivalent general introduction to the second part of the book has been written by Mr George Atkinson, of the Tropical Building Section of the Building Research Station, whom I also have to thank for help and advice when the material on the tropical territories was being collected. In his introduction he discusses, principally, the influence of climate, which overshadows all other considerations when buildings have to be designed for the tropics.

The collection of material for the whole book would have been impossible without the help of those architects in each territory who made a preliminary choice on *The Architectural Review's* behalf, and gathered together photographs and plans from which a final selection could be made by the *Review* editors. Thanks are due to the following for performing this task: Mr Robin Boyd in Australia; Mr Lewis Martin in New Zealand; Mr Walter Manthorpe in Canada; Mr John Godwin in Nigeria; Mr B. G. White and Mr A. E. Crocker in Ghana; Mr R. B. Browning and Mr Richard Hughes in East Africa; Mr P. O. Coltman in Northern Rhodesia; Mr Lloyd Spencer in Southern Rhodesia; Mr J. C. Rose (assisted by Mr J. C. Walker and Mr P. M. Stevens) in the Caribbean; Mr J. Posener in Malaya; Mr P. W. G. Powell in Pakistan; Mr J. L. Middleton and Mr Lincoln Page in Singapore; Mr Peter Morley in the East Indies; Mr Eric Cumine and Mr Stanley Kwok in Hong Kong; Mr F. W. Smith in Fiji.

Finally, thanks are due to the many architects all over the Commonwealth who provided material illustrating their own buildings, and gave permission for it to be published.

J. M. RICHARDS

Contents

Part 1. The Larger Dominions

Part 1. The Larger Dominions: Introduction

THE THREE DOMINIONS with temperate climes which appear in the following pages are Canada, Australia and New Zealand. However, their temperate climes have to be taken with some latitude. Their territories include the icy wastes of Labrador, the steaming rain forests north of Auckland, and the desert of the Australian north from which miraculously rises Mount Isa with the ant-like business of its miners. Their human population includes Eskimos and Maori, their animal population the polar bear and the white whale of Hudson Bay and the platypus of Australia. But where modern architecture goes up, climatic conditions are not so different from those of Europe and the United States. That leaves still enough variety, and it is indeed the differences of climate between the three Dominions, and the corresponding differences in historical growth, in the resulting ethnological situation and in social circumstances, which must be appreciated in order to understand why architecture in Canada, Australia and New Zealand is what it is.

Sizes first: the United Kingdom is 93,000 sq. miles in size; New Zealand 104,000; Australia nearly three million; Canada nearly four – that is more than the United States. Usable space, however, reduces these figures to a fraction in all cases but that of New Zealand.

Population second: Canada has sixteen million inhabitants; Australia nine; New Zealand less than two-and-a-quarter. These populations are mixed, between aboriginal inhabitants and immigrants, the aborigines being, everywhere, a small minority. In Australia there are no more than 50,000 aborigines, in Canada no more than 166,000 Red Indians and Eskimos, in New Zealand 137,000 Maoris, in contrast, for instance, to South Africa where the Native, Asian and coloured population is over twelve million, and the white population not much more than two-and-a-half million. Only the Maoris are fully integrated, but they play no part in the designing of buildings.

Modern building goes on chiefly in cities. If we take cities of over 300,000, over a third of the population of Canada lives in such cities, and half the population of Australia. New Zealand has only one city larger than 300,000 (Auckland), and we must go down to 150,000 to arrive at a ratio of town dwellers to country and country-town dwellers similar to that of the other Dominions.

Finally, cities: Sydney, Melbourne and Montreal have more than a million inhabitants; Toronto comes next with 660,000. All others are below half a million. Sydney is about the size of Detroit, Montreal of Glasgow, and Toronto of Cologne.

The Commonwealth is the most improbable federation. It is welded together by imponderables and yet seems to hold firm. A member may not recognize the Queen and may abhor the National Anthem; a population may be more English than the English (or more Scots than the Scots) and may sing: 'For all her faults I love her still', or it may be frankly anti-English; large groups may speak languages other than English – for instance, French in Canada – and architects may look for their inspiration steadfastly to another country than Britain. And yet they are all coloured pink in the atlas.

What then can be the point of collecting together the new buildings of states and peoples, just because they belong to the Commonwealth, or, in the particular case of the first part of this book, because they are Dominions? One answer is that in all three Dominions it is the population of British origin that builds in a twentieth-century fashion. Only the French Catholic and Protestant churches are a special case and keep with their respective mannerisms on the margin of developments. Another answer is that in all three the architecture that matters is almost without exception the work of resident architects, whereas Chandigarh is a mixed Franco-English affair, and the best in the West Indies, West Africa and Burma is the work of British architects.

Even historically, much allows for comparison between the three Dominions. The architectural story starts French in Canada. Fort de Ramesay in Montreal dates from about 1710. Quebec is purely a French town, with a rampart and bleached shutters, and the churches on the Ile d'Orleans are unmistakably derived from those of France. The British appeared gradually in the great decades of Empire building, and their seal of Georgian red brick was set on Sydney, on Toronto and, with the Anglican Cathedral, even on Quebec. Such churches as St James's, Sydney, and such houses as The Grange at Toronto might be in England or in New England. The architectural beginnings of New Zealand are Early Victorian, and of western Canada, Late Victorian. The Canadian Pacific Railway reached the west coast in 1885; Vancouver, its village terminus, was destroyed by fire in 1886. So the present Vancouver was only begun in 1886. She is the *parvenu* of the Dominion cities, reaching her first 100,000 in 1911. Yet she wears her young wealth and architecture remarkably elegantly.

That, for such cities as Vancouver, the establishment of a twentieth-century style raised no sentimental problem must be obvious. Where there was no tradition the new could be acclaimed with ease. Nor was the situation much different where traditions did exist. They were nowhere as deeply rooted as in England. The mentality of the pioneer, the settler, the immigrant, favours novelty. So the soil ought to have been well suited to an early and a complete victory of modern architecture. As things turned out, in reality, the victory was not earlier than in such hesitant countries as England and America, and, though it was in the end as thorough as in America and far more so than in England, modern architecture was not always what the architectural magazine would illustrate with approval.

A few dates can serve to illustrate the coming of the modern style, a style which had been created in Europe and America between 1900 and 1914, and had left its mark by 1930 well visible at least in the more go-ahead countries. In England, by 1930, there was no more than a handful of buildings which had taken notice of the European architectural revolution; in the United States scarcely any. In Canada the first house in the new style is by Robert Blatter at Sillery, Quebec, and dates from 1932. It is clearly influenced by Le Corbusier. Roy Grounds designed his own house at Mount Eliza, Victoria, in 1933. Mr Plishke's first 'Continental Modern' house in New Zealand dates from 1939, but he had, of course, built in the same style in Austria before.

The vast area of modern architecture which the survey of the following pages will leave unrecorded is spec. builder's housing. This, which in England still looks to Neo-Tudor and in England and the United States to Neo-Georgian, grows in all three Dominions in a modernistic vernacular, bright, neat and fairly acceptable if it were not for the almost total absence of planning. Exclaves of planning, such as the bit of civic centre at Lower Hutt near Wellington, or the much larger and more consistent use-zoning at Don Mills outside Toronto, are so rare that one takes them more seriously than one would in Europe. The standard is the never-ending suburb of bungalows, widely spaced in well-to-do, crammed together in poorer, districts. Never do they make visual sense. They look gay and are well looked after, with their ice-cream shades and their streamlined windows. Modern clichés have been absorbed naturally and vulgarized with disarming success. Only in Canada does low-price housing rise higher than bungalow height. The detached dominates everywhere, and that again defeats any attempts at visual planning. Public housing is rare. These are countries of free enterprise. New Zealand, pro-portionally speaking, has most governmental enterprise in housing. Hutt was developed, not too successfully, on garden-suburb principles, and groups of three-storey flats, also built by the Government Architect's department, appear in many places. Of late, even high-rise residential blocks have been undertaken. High blocks of flats in Canada mean high rents, and Toronto has some where it also means a high quality of architecture. But vertical accents in horizontal estates are absent everywhere. There is opposition to the mixed developments which England has, in the 'fifties, developed so successfully. Where high flats appear, too many appear in one area, and the high office block, which in the large cities has become a matter of course, can also rise pretty well unchecked. The standard dress is the curtain-wall, a minimum solution as unreasonable in the winter cold of Montreal as in the summer heat of Toronto. Little independent thought has gone into the problem of marrying modern form with conditions of climate. But little has also been done about this in the United States. Air-conditioning is an unimaginative answer and, moreover, the curtain-wall has more often been copied in the Dominions than the air-conditioning.

That Toronto should look to Detroit and Chicago, and Vancouver to Seattle, San Francisco and Los Angeles is nothing surprising. But that, throughout the three Dominions, England as a source of inspiration has been eclipsed by America calls for some thinking. Sentimental ties with the homeland have not snapped anywhere. When it comes to juries, to a fair judgment on national or international matters of architectural design, the best English experts were called to Canberra to redress the damage done to Walter Burley Griffin's plan, and to Sydney and Toronto to decide who should build the Opera House and the City Hall, and Robert Matthew was commissioned to build New Zealand House in Pall Mall. Moreover, most of the professors of architecture (e.g. in Melbourne, Sydney and Toronto) were trained in Britain. One would expect that they would determine the direction in which their students would look. But that is not so and, perhaps, could not be so.

Once again, for Canada the proximity to the United States was too close to be resisted. The Canadian speaks of 'gasoline' not of 'petrol', of 'high school' and 'sidewalk', of 'highway' and 'subway'. As for Australia and New Zealand, it ought to be remembered that their world is centred in the Pacific, not the Atlantic. California is nearer than England and in climate and ways of life more akin.

So here is a situation which allows for the three Dominions to be seen together. The architects who now lead are their own, not, as a rule, immigrants. Their roots are in Britain, but their eyes are on the United States. They are not hemmed in by tradition, by the preservation of worthwhile older buildings, and so they enjoy a mental and material freedom which may well be envied. Have they then succeeded in absorbing a style created and developed by others, in making it their own and in creating work that can stand by the side of the best abroad? The following pages present the material to answer this question; but any answer must remain personal. If, on the strength of this introduction, certain names may be put forward as candidates, I would propose John Parkin and Charles E. Pratt in Canada, Roy Grounds and Walter Bunning in Australia and, perhaps, Werner Plishke and the high slabs by Gordon Wilson, late Government Architect, in New Zealand.

NIKOLAUS PEVSNER

AUSTRALIAN CULTURE IS SOMETHING like a sturdy little boat battling across lonely waters surging with cross-currents from Europe and America. The boat is equipped with a strong thrashing screw but as yet an ineffectual rudder. In the case of modern architecture the three propulsive elements in the culture are conveniently, if atypically, represented by the three men, all now dead, who struggled to bring the movement to life shortly before the first World War. Firstly, the Englishman, Robert Haddon, a Romantic-functionalist inheriting a little from Morris and Mackintosh: a scholastic man, fond of his new land but always nostalgic for the Old Country. Secondly, the quiet American, Walter Burley Griffin, direct from Taliesin, radiating gentle warmth, organic theory and democratic New World idealism. Thirdly, the Australian, Harold Desbrowe Annear, who was born in Ballarat in 1866 when it was still hardly more than a gold-rush canvas town. Annear never left Australia. He was impatient with such tuition as he could get in Melbourne. He was an experimenter, improviser, inventor of architectural gadgetry. He was self-confident and rebellious. He ridiculed 'good taste' and traditions, preferring what he imagined were his own answers, whatever their faults. He was inconsistent, unstable and not altogether reliable, but among his best works are some which deserve passing recognition alongside the European and Chicagoean pioneers of the movement. (Not that Annear, working in isolation from hearsay and first principles, would have known the others' names or expected recognition outside the smarter streets of Toorak or Portsea where he worked.)

The antipodean isolation has since been modified by radio and jets, but still the three elements are to be found separately, each in a fairly pure state. The Old World is now represented architecturally by a persistent, if slowly shrinking, streak of conservatism that diverts attention from form to detail. The results of this are never exactly academic, but, on the other hand, not quite as dowdy as Europe at her stodgiest. The New World is represented by a more than usually hysterical worship of the American image: 'Austericanism', it has been called. This leads to violent primary-hued delinquency – not clever enough to be fashionably smart, but, on the other hand, never quite as mad as Miami. The physical isolation of Australia from her spiritual sisters of the West is not in fact felt strongly enough to be valuable. It is not sharp enough to free architects to work out their own solutions. The oceans have worked as a valve permitting only a one-way passage of ideas: inwards

B

always from the higher-pressure areas, continuously inflating feelings of inadequacy, or frustration, among the local practitioners of all arts. The supremacy of the importation is a popular concept against which the Annear spirit of indiscipline has rebelled at intervals, and has produced one vital strain of modern Australian building.

But the average unintrospective Australian architect and his client are not, of course, disturbed by the action of the valve. There is no serious suggestion of aggressive artistic nationalism. Any Australian flavour in everyday building appears to be involuntary, in some obvious ways related to the qualities which visitors usually discover in the Australian human character. He is (observers often say) easy-going to an extent which exasperates urgent North Americans and exact Central Europeans. 'Near enough' is the national philosophy: a deliberate cult of anti-finesse, of outbackmanship. But (they admit) he answers up to challenges. He is resourceful, an ingenious improviser, a born mechanic, the sort of fellow you like to have close by in an emergency. These qualities colour, to some extent, all the styles of Australian building. They help to produce a background that is practical, unstylish, technically advanced, casual in detail and often hideously garish. And they produce the opposite: buildings that recognize the existence of a challenge, of an artistic emergency for a rich and lazy young nation which could quite easily be swamped entirely by imported mass-produced ideas.

Sensitive Australian laymen, aware of this general danger, and searching architecture for a 'National Style', look hopefully to the colonial building of the early nineteenth century. Here was a displaced, delayed, diminutive Georgian with all the charm of diminution and anachronism, and just enough subtle peculiarities to mark it from other and earlier Georgian work. The domestic variant was quite distinctive: a low, hipped shingle roof, later corrugated iron, pulled down all round a white house, like a wide hat brim shading the long evenly-spaced windows. Australians can see – though it is less perceptible to visitors – a continuing tradition based on this relaxed and random form. The uncrowded single-storey, wide sun-shading eaves, and extroversion, combined with the peculiarities of the kiln-dried native timbers and the cheapness of Australian steel, still produce in unselfconscious construction a sort of adopted indigenous character.

Australia has many things in common with Sweden and California, including a filial feeling for the twentieth century. Thus, a fairly accurate idea of modern Australia may be gained by imagining an under-populated California. It is hardly surprising that the buildings of both regions have been similar for more than a hundred years. The climate, colouring and social background are similar, and both discovered gold and galvanized iron about the same time. On the other hand, Australia may be pictured even better by thinking of Sweden and then imagining the extreme opposite. Australian taste is all peaks and valleys. No landscapes have been outraged more wantonly than the untidy olive and ochre sites of most Australian towns. The first move of the land exploiters still is to remove all trace of native growth. Fevered advertising, frank or subconscious, almost submerges architecture in the commercial areas, and every sensitive building is all but smothered by its neighbours. The one architectural vice Australia need not fear is monotony.

But the mess on the surface does not convey the whole activity and gives no indication of the individual soul-searching which accompanies a young nation trying earnestly to know its own mind. If the outrage is wilder than usual, so is the outcry against it. Protest and criticism is at least as lively as anywhere, and architecture is a popular art. It is popular because patronage of it is within reach of almost everyone sometimes in his life; if not in his business, then in the separate suburban cottage often shaped individually for him in defiance of technical advances or business efficiency. The designs of big public projects are widely discussed, architectural criticism is given space in the daily press, and the intricacies of contemporary domestic architecture are a standard butt of television comedians.

The people look to the architect for stimulation and excitement, and, at the present time, the architects are as uncertain as they are in any other country as to how they should respond. The younger architect still clings to the faith that there is rational justification for his modern eclecticism. He absorbs the influences of Europe and America separately through the magazines and in travel taken as soon as possible after graduation. His first trip takes him to Europe, concentrating on Italy, Scandinavia and Great Britain. His second trip is to the U.S.A. He is looking for practice rather than theory, and on returning home he finds the *Forum* more helpful than the *Architectural Review*, and both more rewarding than any of the local architectural journals. Thus, numerous curtain walls are rising in the bigger cities from fifteen towards thirty floors – as clean, conformist and comfortable as ever they were in New York. Then there are Australian versions of all the mid-century mannerisms from Brutalism to Edward Stone, and eager young men who imitate early Wright, convinced that they are original, constructive humanists. There are also some quite free-thinkers and those whose first trip overseas is to Japan and Australia's northern Asian neighbours. And there are, finally, those of the Annear spirit: the architectural bushrangers. It would be fun to think that these last are growing in number, strength and maturity, but the truth seems to be the contrary. The rebels are fading away as Australia gets more populous, prosperous, industrialized and confident. The exciting things in Australian modern architecture were, until recently, isolated experiments done with little more than sticks, wires, space and unencouraged enthusiasm. But, already, the last continent is losing its innocence.

ROBIN BOYD

Australia

Facing page (left): office building, Sydney (architects, Stephenson and Turner), the headquarters of Unilever in Australia, in Macquarie Street, between Government House and the harbour, and the last large building before Benelong Point, the site of the future opera house. It is a 16-storey rectangular block with its two long faces slightly curved. Services and lifts are concentrated at the southern end, leaving the remaining floor-space free except for one staircase near the north end. The floors are cantilevered outwards from two rows of reinforced concrete columns. The glass panels between windows are etched on the inside to match the floor-slabs. No windows open, the building being air-conditioned by four plants which can be separately operated to deal with the irregular concentration of sunshine on the four façades.

Facing page (right): office building, Melbourne (architects, Bates, Smart and McCutcheon), the Australian headquarters of Imperial Chemical Industries; an 18-storey block at the east end of the city. Above ground it occupies less than half the site area, leaving room for a garden and car-park at ground level, but the whole site is excavated to provide two basements containing stores, services and a 65-car garage. Construction is lightweight steel frame with curtain wall of aluminium and blue-grey, heat-toughened glass. The building is fully air-conditioned.

Above: office building in North Sydney (architects, Stephenson and Turner), an 11-storey block for commercial letting with lock-up shops on the ground floor. The office space is planned round a central service core and is air-conditioned. The structure is steel frame with concrete slab floors giving flush ceilings. The east façade consists of an aluminium curtain wall with fixed windows and porcelain enamel panels. The other three façades are in light coloured brickwork with continuous aluminium windows.

Left: insurance offices, Adelaide (architects, Bates, Smart and McCutcheon; associate architects, Lawson, Cheesman and Doley); for the Mutual Life and Citizens' Assurance Company. The building overlooks a large city square and is set back on its side to admit daylight on three sides. It is air-conditioned to a special design to meet the high heat-loading on the long east and west façades. It has a light-weight steel frame, steel deck floors and fire-proofing of lightweight concrete. Curtain walls are of glass in aluminium frames with aluminium brise-soleil.

Anzac House, College Street, Sydney (architects, Bunning and Madden),
a five-storey office building serving as headquarters for returned soldiers'
organizations and as a memorial for two world wars. It was the result of a
competition held in 1948. The ground floor contains an auditorium seating
350, a large foyer and a war-memorial hall. Above are offices either side of a
central corridor on an L-shaped plan. Balconies 5 ft. deep provide shade on
the west façade. The structure is steel-framed with reinforced concrete floor
and roof slabs. External cladding is travertine with grey terracotta panels
under windows. Above: the exterior. Below, left: the memorial hall.
Below, right: the auditorium.

Australia

Bush Hospital, Beulah, Victoria (architects, Peter and Dione McIntyre), a small, six-bed hospital designed for almost desert climatic conditions. The structure is designed around the central mast supporting the rain-water tank, from which also radiate the aluminium slats of the umbrella-shaped false roof, which protects the main roof from sun-heat yet permits air to flow over it. Aluminium slats also shade the side walls, with a four-foot air-space between walls and slats. Below: the construction of the roof louvres from the 'service court' in the centre of the building, with the rain-water tank on the left.

Factory offices at Lane Cove, an outer suburb of Sydney (architects, Edwards, Madigan and Torzillo). The offices occupy the main ground floor with staff amenities in the basement. They are steel framed on a reinforced concrete raft slab with timber roof covered in asbestos felt and aluminium foil.

23

Left: insurance offices, Sydney (architects, Peddle, Thorp and Walker), for the Australian Mutual Provident Society: a 26-storey block (the tallest in the city) in Sydney's ancient Circular Quay area, dominating the waterfront. At ground level there is a large public area sheltered by the overhanging first floor. The ground floor contains an auditorium seating 260. Car-parks are in two basements. The air-conditioned office space is uninterrupted by columns.

Academy of Science building, Canberra (architects, Grounds, Romberg and Boyd), a headquarters for the representative body of Australian scientists. The circular building contains a conference hall, reception rooms, reading rooms, exhibition gallery and offices (see opposite page). The conference hall is in the centre with the other accommodation on two floors round it, separated by a circular corridor on the ground floor. The main entrance and foyer are at the north and the large Fellows' room at the south. The overhang of the dome shields the windows from direct sunlight.

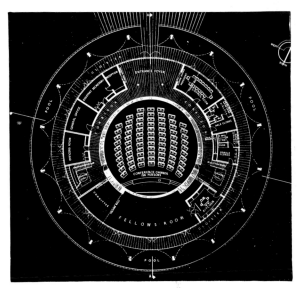

Above: Academy of Science building, Canberra (see also facing page). The air-conditioned conference hall (top, left) is 64 ft. in diameter. The structure is monolithic shell concrete, 3-in. thick, resting at sixteen points on a concrete ring which forms the base of a water-filled moat round the building (top, right). The dome (bottom, left) is sheathed in copper. Bottom right· main floor plan.

Right: Church at Dalkeith, a suburb of Perth, W.A. (architects, F. G. B. Hawkins and Desmond Sands). It seats 340. The floor of the nave has a slight slope to improve sight-lines. Walls are brick and concrete and the roof steel and timber covered with tiles.

Music Bowl, Melbourne (architects, Yuncken, Freeman brothers, Griffiths and Simpson). The roof, which covers stage, orchestra and the front rows of seats, was not designed primarily to give shelter but to deflect the sound of nearby traffic (see top illustration, facing page). It is supported by twin steel masts, cased in glass fibre with ball-and-socket joints at the foot to permit movement. The main cable passing over the tops of the masts is 568 ft. in length and it weighs 40 tons. The roof-covering is $\frac{1}{2}$-in. plywood, faced with aluminium, bolted to secondary transverse cables. The joints have polythene and nylon washers to suppress sound caused by movement of the structure. Dressing-rooms are fitted in below the stage.

Above: Music Bowl, Melbourne (see facing page).

Below: restaurant at Dalkeith, W. Australia (architects, Forbes and Fitzhardinge). It has a domed roof in shell concrete, supported at three points forming an equilateral triangle with 61-ft. sides and rising to 16 ft. at the crown. The shell was poured continuously in ten hours. The underside of the dome is sprayed with asbestos. The restaurant and outdoor terraces together seat forty, and adjoin a swimming-pool.

Wilson Hall, Melbourne University (architects, Bates, Smart and McCutcheon), used for conferring degrees and other ceremonies. It replaced a Gothic-style hall burnt down in 1952. The main floor seats 1,000, with a further 300 seats in a gallery sloping back over the entrance foyer. Construction is steel frame. The eastern wall is heat-absorbent glass in aluminium framing; the other walls largely brick.

Olympic Pool, Melbourne (architects, Borland, McIntyre, Murphy and Murphy), built to house the swimming and diving sections of the 1956 Olympic Games. 6,000 spectators can be accommodated on two tiers of seats whose outward-sloping beam-supports are tied together across the pool by diamond-shaped roof trusses. The only external structural elements are stabilising guy-rods.

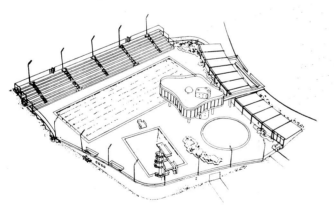

Swimming pools at Brisbane (architect, James Birrell).
The group of pools, with grandstand, changing
accommodation and café, was built in 1959 by the city
council. It includes a main pool 165 ft. by 60 ft., a
diving pool 90 ft. by 60 ft. and a circular paddling
pool, with a total maximum accommodation for 610
people (two-thirds in the water at one time). The
grandstand seats 1,200, and there is a sun-bathing area
for 200. The site, at Gregory Terrace, is on the outskirts
of the city near one of its major approaches. The
grandstand is terraced into the slope along the north-
eastern side. There are views over the city and the
adjoining Victoria Park from the roof of the café (shown
above, with the diving pool in foreground and the main
pool and grandstand beyond). Right: the reinforced
concrete diving tower.

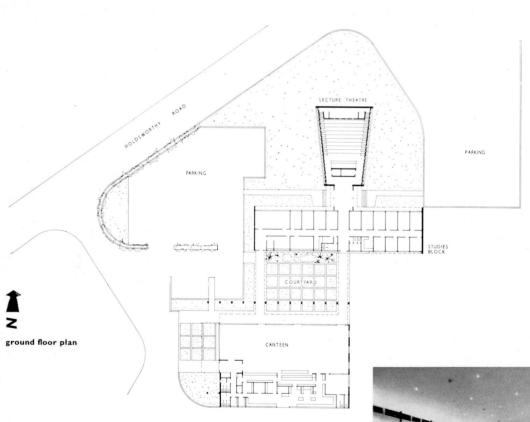

ground floor plan

A group of three buildings for the Australian Atomic Energy Commission at Lucas Heights, Sydney (architects, Bunning and Madden), consisting of a lecture theatre, a study block and a staff canteen (top of page and right). The canteen, serving 300 people, is 26 ft. high with a barrel roof hung from 13 bowstring steel arches, exposed internally and painted black, spanning 72 ft. between concrete buttresses at ground level. The ribbed aluminium roof follows the same curve.

Below: the whole group of atomic science buildings, at Sydney, with the canteen (see facing page) on the right, the study block, containing 13 studies, library, conference-room and offices, in the centre and the lecture-theatre on the left. Above: close-up of the lecture-theatre, which seats 150, is artificially lighted and has side walls of pre-cast concrete louvres edged with timber, and brick end walls, all framed in black-painted pressed metal.

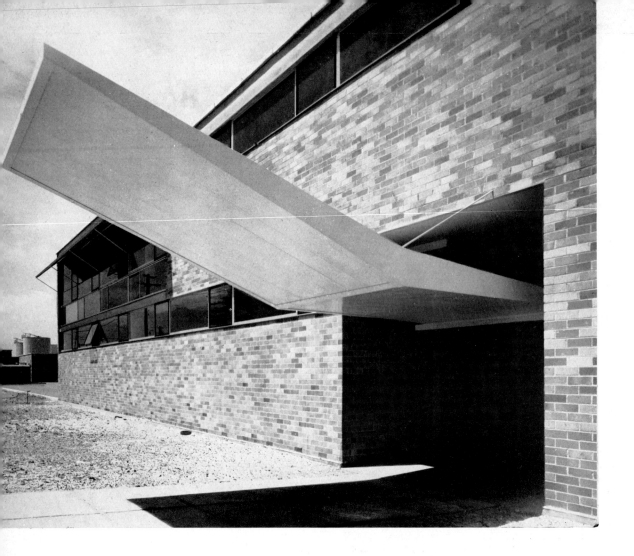

Welfare building for an oil refinery's distribution centre, Banksmeadow, New South Wales (architect, Harry Seidler). The ground floor has workshops at one end and lavatories and lockers at the other. Between them is a passage through the building, the entrance to which is marked by a cantilevered reinforced concrete canopy (above). Upper-floor lockers, lavatories and showers are reached by stairs from this passage. The remainder of the upper floor is occupied by a diningroom, seating 120, reached by an outside stair. Floors and roof are flatslab reinforced concrete, cantilevered from circular columns. Outside walls are 11-in. cavity brick. The diningroom is fully glazed on north and south sides, the north being protected from the sun by a sloping awning of pressed steel.

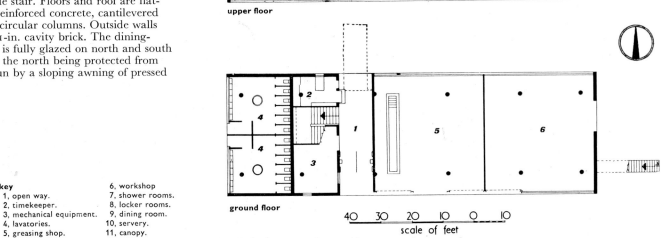

upper floor

ground floor

key
1, open way.
2, timekeeper.
3, mechanical equipment.
4, lavatories.
5, greasing shop.
6, workshop
7, shower rooms.
8, locker rooms.
9, dining room.
10, servery.
11, canopy.

scale of feet
40 30 20 10 0 10

House at Turramurra, N.S.W. (architects, Archer, Mortlock and Murray), on a typical bushland site on Sydney's fashionable North Shore on to which the house is designed to fit as unobtrusively as possible.

Below, left: house at Wahroonga, N.S.W. (architects, John Allen and Russell C. Jack), for the latter's occupation. The site is rock-covered and heavily wooded with eucalyptus trees. A small watercourse crosses it diagonally. The house has a timber-framed structure with twin columns supporting main beams at floor and roof level. Internal and external brick-work is painted a sand colour; other internal and external walls are vertical mahogany boarding. Windows are Queensland maple. Right: house at Templestowe, Victoria (architect, Kenneth McDonald), a small hillside house for a doctor and his wife and occasional guest, planned round a central service core with internal bathroom lit and ventilated through a window above roof level. Construction is timber and brick with roof covering of aluminium foil.

Flats at Toorak, Victoria (architects, Grounds, Romberg and Boyd). This development in a suburb of Melbourne comprises four flats and a house for Roy Grounds (see facing page). The flats are built down the slope of a hill and are planned to provide privacy. The living-room (above) of each flat faces on to its own enclosed courtyard.

Roy Grounds's own house at Toorak (see facing page). It is square in plan with a circular courtyard in the centre. Construction is load-bearing brick, concrete slab floors, which are heated, and timber framed flat roofs. Window sashes are aluminium set in a structural frame of Victorian mountain ash.

House at Melbourne (architects, Grounds, Romberg and Boyd), built for Mr Robin Boyd's own occupation – see description on facing page. Above: the parents' end seen from the courtyard. Left: the family living-room (the lower of the two rooms seen in the top illustration) showing the staircase and, beyond it, the cupboard fitment that partly screens off the kitchen.

Above: The parents' bed-sitting room in the house at Melbourne, also shown on the facing page, looking east towards the balcony and courtyard beyond. The house stands on a narrow site surrounded by high buildings. The separation of parents' and children's accommodation was desired, and these are planned at either end of a garden courtyard, with the parents' bedroom on an upper floor taking advantage of the only view – over suburban roofs to distant hills. The timber roofs of the two ends are continuous, except for the central opening over the courtyard. They are carried on ¾-in. steel cables tied to steel frames at the intervals and supported intermediately on the timber posts of the glazed walls. Other walls are brick, reinforced by steel tubes in the cavities.

key. 1, car-port. 2, children's bedrooms. 3, children's sitting room. 4, children's shower. 5, courtyard. 6, family living room. 7, kitchen. 8, balcony. 9, parents' bed-sitting room. 10, bathroom. 11, entrance.

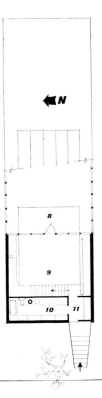

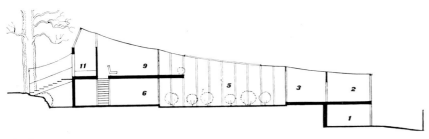

Section

ground floor

first floor

House at Roseville Chase, N.S.W. (architect, Maurice
Morrison). Sited in a natural hollow, back from the
highway, with views in the opposite direction, the living-
room therefore faces north and east over a pool (above).
There are two bedrooms. It has a steel frame resting on a
concrete floor-slab suspended over the rocky slope.
Walls (non structural) are concrete externally and painted
plywood internally. Ceilings are boarded. The bathroom
is top-lit. Below: the living room.

House at Turramurra, New South Wales (architect, Harry Seidler) seen, above, from the north. It stands on the edge of a public bushland reserve, and is raised off the ground with all rooms facing north to exploit the view. The main accommodation is on the first floor: kitchen and bathroom are in the centre, back-to-back, separating the dining and living quarters on the east from the main-bedroom on the west. The ground floor is mostly open, but in the centre is a spare-bedroom and shower. The car-port beneath one end of the overhang is hidden from the garden by a louvred screen (shown in the view above). The structure has four supporting columns which, by means of diagonal steel-pipe hangers, carry the horizontal frame. The infill is brick below and timber for the upper level. The walls are of timber faced with vertical boarding. Windows are steel-framed in timber. Left: from the west, showing the open ground floor and the external stair leading to the terrace which runs along the south side.

House at Vermont, Victoria (architect, Kenneth McDonald); a low-cost house of 900 sq. ft. for a couple with one child. Sited among gum-trees to make the most of distant mountain views, it has an open living area, completely separated from the sleeping sections. Construction is largely timber with roof covered with aluminium foil. Internal walls are cypress pine running vertically.

House at Pymble, N.S.W. (see facing page).

Above and on facing page: house at Pymble,
N.S.W. (architect Harry Seidler). A sloping
3-acre site with a view to the south
determined the split-level plan with super-
imposed living and bedrooms both facing the
view. The single-slope timber roof has a white
mineral surface visible from the approach
side. Walls are brick or local sandstone with
extensions acting as retaining walls and
giving privacy to outdoor spaces. Floors are
flat concrete slabs. Living rooms are lined
internally with vertical timber boarding. The
house has underfloor electric heating.

Australia

House at Northbridge, Sydney (architect, Harry Seidler) on a narrow site sloping towards a harbour inlet. The house is placed below a rocky ridge that crossed the site, and is reached by a bridge. A covered car-port is on the upper level, alongside the road – see view from road (left). All rooms face north towards the view. The living area (below) is open and is in part carried up two storeys, so that a study on the top floor forms a balcony. Also on the top floor (not shown on the plans) are two bedrooms and a bathroom. Construction is brick, painted off-white, with steel beams and columns.

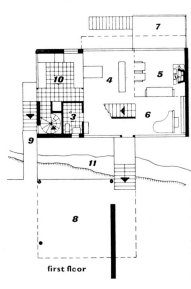

first floor

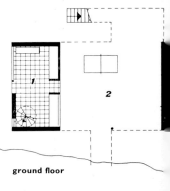

ground floor

key

1, laundry and storage.
2, outdoor play.
3, wash room.
4, dining room.
5, living room.
6, music room.
7, terrace.
8, car park.
9, service.
10, kitchen.
11, rock led

New Zealand

NEW ZEALAND IS ONE-THIRTIETH the size of Australia; but that figure is deceiving; for whereas Australia has immense wastes within her boundaries, New Zealand is on the whole cultivated throughout, even if Central Otago carries only one sheep on every five (and sometimes ten) acres. The country lives on agriculture, cattle-breeding and sheep-rearing, and it lives comfortably on that – comfortably in the sense that everyone has enough and few have too much. There are no riches and there is no poverty, and there is a welfare organization only matched in Britain, and certainly of longer standing than in Britain. All these conditions find their reflection in architecture. Climatic differences are curiously little represented, although the range goes from areas of sub-tropical rain forest, by way of moderately rainy areas much like England and Scotland, to alpine and fjord areas. The bush is not what it is in South Africa; it is dense growth of forest, with or without tangled undergrowth according to latitude. In the forests down in the south-west corner of the South Island, south of Milford Sound, there are still unexplored patches. But mostly the countryside is inhabited, sparsely of course, and houses – except for some small Maori holdings – are clean and well looked after. Urban population amounts to over 40 per cent. if inhabitants of towns of over 100,000 are called urban. There are no slums; there is only overcrowding of the same small, not at all neglected, bungalows which, not quite so densely sited, make up other suburbs as well. New houses are bungalows almost without exception. They are of timber, with a verandah, brightly painted and as a rule as innocent of architectural values as are spec.-builders' houses at home. But they are never imitation-Tudor, or indeed imitation-anything, except, of course, imitation-modern-clichés. If they could recently be called an 'ingratiating chaos' the adjective refers to their cheerful appearance individually, the noun to their siting and placing. There is no town-planning worth speaking of, either in central or in suburban areas. In central areas, in fact, there is none; in the suburbs the Government Architect has occasionally tried to group bungalow housing by means of winding streets into a kind of garden-city pattern (Hutt near Wellington). But the bungalows, his building components, defeat him. Auckland, the largest town, is only the size of Nottingham. Wellington and Christchurch correspond about to Aberdeen; Dunedin is no bigger than Luton.

Everybody wants a house of his own, and after a few years the new immigrant can afford one. New blocks of flats are exceedingly rare and almost exclusively built by the Government Architect, either in groups of three and four storeys, or, here and there, in high slabs looking as good as most of their European patterns. Of these high slabs one was built at Wellington before the war; a second at Wellington and one at Auckland, both taller and more exciting in appearance, are recent.

High buildings are all but absent in the centres of cities too. Auckland has one slab of Government offices recently completed, and Wellington is going to have a fifteen-storey point-block of Government offices. That is, so far, pretty well all. It is perhaps the most characteristic feature of the architectural situation in New Zealand that the Government Architect's Department is responsible for nearly all the major work in the country, and that, in addition, the department, under its head Gordon Wilson, who died prematurely two years ago, represented the spearhead of modern enterprise instead of being safely in the rear as one would expect in Europe, and as is, for instance, the case in South Africa. Office buildings which fall to private architects are never as big as they can be in Australia, nor are factories. The biggest office buildings were built between the two wars and are a minor variant of American manners. Of work of the last few years, Mr Plishke's Massey House at Wellington is an exception in scale as well as careful detailing. The same applies to Mr Plishke's house for Dr Sutch, an exception in New Zealand private houses. This loving pursuit of the refined detail may well be the architect's Viennese heritage.

Most of the other modern architects are New Zealand-trained, or have gone through English or American schools. Those who have not, try to travel; but scholarships and grants are too costly to be possible and private travel naturally even more so. The respect for England is great, and emotional ties are as a rule admitted, but the relations are platonic. The majority of the work of the younger architects is small private houses of timber, and for these England has nothing to offer. Looking across the Pacific pays better, and Californian houses in the journals are pondered over with more profit than English ones. A good deal of ingenuity goes into planning, and this ingenuity is needed; for the client is never rich. In England, without any doubt, he would buy himself an old house and redecorate it; he would never be a client. Old houses in New Zealand have not yet acquired a period value. Preservationism is completely absent; too much so, one is inclined to say. Apart from such historical monuments as Maori meeting houses, some Maori Christian churches and the early mission buildings of Bishop Selwyn, nothing is accepted as worth keeping. None of the extremely pretty farmhouses, surrounded by verandas with fretwork or cast-iron trim, is excepted. So architects have work, but they don't grow rich on it. Lack of means is often apparent in the detailing, although a certain crudity is called straightforwardness and, at least by some of the most thoughtful young architects, set up as a new-country feature in opposition to the old-men's fussiness at home. It sounds convincing at first, though California is not all that old and yet is quite capable of taking its details seriously.

Of public buildings, schools and universities are usually served by the Government Architect. Several major jobs have recently been completed, such as the Dental School at Dunedin and the Department of Engineering at Christchurch. Some of the new hotels of the semi-governmental tourist organization, on the other hand, have been handed on to private architects. Those at Milford Sound and the Hermitage, just in front of Mount Cook, the highest mountain of New Zealand, are excellent jobs, light and fresh and well furnished and perhaps more inspired by Italy than by America. Inspiration from England in this field is, alas, out of the question. The new airport at Christchurch is also privately handled, by Mr Paul Pascoe, and is equally satisfactory. Ecclesiastical work is on the whole disappointing, except for the famous pre-war chapel of Waiho, where the Southern Alps behind a glass wall make an unforgettable reredos, and its progeny, and except for Mr McCoy's Roman Catholic buildings in Otago and farther south.

There is only one school of architecture in New Zealand – at Auckland. It has recently established a town-planning department, with English staffing. The department is going to have an uphill fight. Physical planning is a latter-day activity. It is also a matter of subtlety. Pioneers don't need it. It follows after you have settled down for good and accepted conditions as stable. This not even the United States has done yet, if one excepts road-planning which is not town-planning. How could it have established itself in New Zealand, where the countryside is vast in comparison to population, and the towns are without exception not vast? So, town-planning would be primarily visual planning, and visual planning would be viewed with misunderstanding and even suspicion by the laymen, and might well be looked at by architects themselves as an old-man's game, just as much as sensitive detailing.

NIKOLAUS PEVSNER

Flats at Auckland city (see facing page).

New Zealand

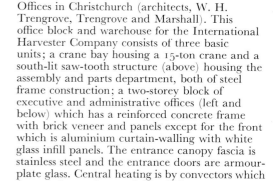

Offices in Christchurch (architects, W. H. Trengrove, Trengrove and Marshall). This office block and warehouse for the International Harvester Company consists of three basic units; a crane bay housing a 15-ton crane and a south-lit saw-tooth structure (above) housing the assembly and parts department, both of steel frame construction; a two-storey block of executive and administrative offices (left and below) which has a reinforced concrete frame with brick veneer and panels except for the front which is aluminium curtain-walling with white glass infill panels. The entrance canopy fascia is stainless steel and the entrance doors are armour-plate glass. Central heating is by convectors which form an integral part of the window design.

Facing page: flats at Auckland (F. G. F. Sheppard, Government Architect). The site is in Auckland city and the building, which has 89 flats (75 two-level, two-bedroom maisonettes and 14 bed-sitting rooms on the ground floor), is of reinforced concrete wall and slab construction, without beams or columns. The use of concrete for domestic work is new to New Zealand, and great trouble has been taken in these flats with the use of fair-faced concrete to provide a smooth finish with true alignment and free from blemishes.

Showroom at Napier (architect, Maurice Smith), a complex structure for a concrete company, housing offices and services at one end and becoming (without any defined point of transition) a display of materials and techniques at the other. The part illustrated, while largely a display structure, also serves as a car-port, and the flooring is 'on view' as well as in use.

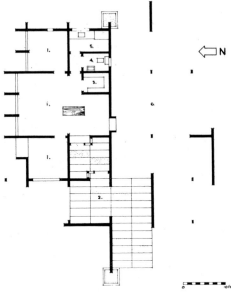

plan of concrete showrooms

Below (right): house at Queen Charlotte Sound, near Picton (architects, Porter and Martin). A holiday house built on a slope in a cup of the hills. The section follows the slope of the hill, making possible a boat-shelter on the lower level. The external sheathing is of vertical shiplap pine boards which were run through boiling tar oil before being fixed; living room walls are covered with the same boards with a satin clear varnish.

Below: house at Wellington (architects, Gabites and Beard), on the bush-clad slopes of Mount Johnston. It was initially built up on columns and bracing walls and occupied on the upper floor only; as the family has grown the bedrooms below have been put into use. The structure is of Douglas fir posts and beams, bolted with Heart Rimu floor joists, Pinus Radiata ceiling joists and sarking and Heart Matai decking. Weatherboards are red stained and oiled, with black painted vertical facings and window frames and fascias painted white. Inside there are Pinus Radiata close-boarded ceilings with a clear finish; the beams and columns of Douglas fir are stained red.

House at Raumati (architects, Plishke and Firth). This house, of 2,000 square feet, has separate bathrooms for parents, boys and guests, a factor above the average in standard for New Zealand, though in view of the lack of domestic help, the highly-mechanised kitchen is not. Timber is used for the structure since it provides greater elasticity in case of earthquake. The system of electric ceiling heating was used here for the first time in New Zealand.

ground floor plan: house at Raumati

Demonstration house at Titirangi (architect, Gerhard Rosenberg), built to demonstrate economy in the use of timber, of which about 2,500 board feet are used, and the value of some new structural ideas and materials. The outside is of block veneer which takes care of earthquake stresses, leaving the framing to carry only the roof load. The roof has exposed rafters of Oregon pine.

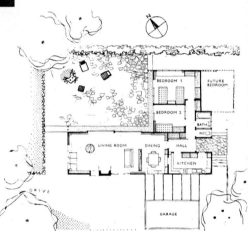

House at Belmont (architects, Plishke and Firth), an L-plan villa with provision for enlargement at the back of the bedroom wing (see plan). All the main rooms face on to a paved court to the north-west, which is the sun-trap orientation for New Zealand. Below: the living room.

House at Milford, Auckland (architects, Juriss, Penman and Wilson). On a flat site 100 yards from the beach, it was designed for a yachtsman owner with two children. Exterior walls are of hollow concrete block painted inside and out. Waxed matai ply is used for furniture and panelling. Roof framing is all of Oregon pine. Heating is by a coke-burning space-heater.

Brick and timber houses perched among the hills containing the suburbs of Wellington. In the foreground is a house designed by Anthony Treadwell.

House at Wellington (architects, Plishke and Firth).
On a steep hill overlooking Wellington Harbour and
planned on different levels in order to get the
maximum benefit from sun and view. Courtyards and
terraces are closely related to the living areas to
provide outdoor living protected from the wind. The
structure is a wood frame; the dark stone for the east
terrace was brought 500 miles from Auckland, while
the golden sandstone which paves the patio and
continues into the gallery and hall (see lower
illustration, facing page), was brought 2,000 miles
by sea from Australia.

Another view of the house at Wellington, by Plishke
and Firth (see facing page). Below: the hall.

Flats in Dorset Street, Christchurch (architect, F. M. Warren). The building comprises eight flats, four on each floor. The four ground-floor flats each have their own private garden surrounded by high walls. Walls are of load-bearing concrete block, painted white inside and out; the roof is timber-framed covered with corrugated iron, with ceilings following the pitch of the roof. Heating is by free-standing Norwegian stoves, set on quarry tile bases.

Offices at Wellington (architects, Plishke and Firth).
Built for the New Zealand Government Boards for
meat and milk, which represent the main industries
in New Zealand, apart from that of wool. The
building, facing Lambton Quay, is seven storeys high.
The structural framework has been kept free of the
enclosing curtain walls, which have deep mullions to
give texture and depth to the façade. A curved wall
in the Dairy Board room is panelled with totara burr
veneer, obtained from the root of the now rare totara
tree; it is made up of 390 individual pieces.

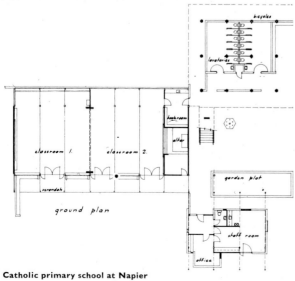

School at Napier (architects, John Scott and Hammond Hastings). This Catholic primary girls' school was built on a clear flat two-acre site to accommodate 200 pupils, with facilities for 400 when extra classrooms are built. The plan is based on the open corridor or verandah system; three separate buildings are grouped to form an open court; the two elevated classrooms cover sheltered play areas. Screen walls of concrete block wander and infill between columns. Roofs are of scissor type, self-supporting timber trusses.

Catholic primary school at Napier

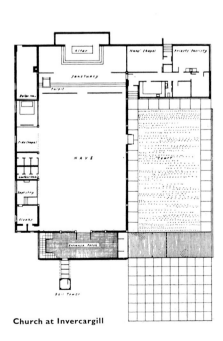

Top (left): church at Invercargill (architect, E. J. McCoy). Dedicated to St. Therese of Lisieux, this concrete-framed church has a straight-forward hall-like interior, flanked on one side by baptistery, confessionals, and side-chapels. On the other side is a grass court (to the right in photograph) at whose head is a subsidiary wing containing sacristy and nuns' chapel. (See plan on right.)

Top (right): St. Martin's Presbyterian Church, Christchurch (architects, Plishke and Firth). It stands in a suburban area, and is designed both for worship and as a social centre. For this purpose the rear block of seating can be partitioned off from the main body of the church. The structure is composite; the free-standing exterior columns are steel, the rest of reinforced concrete; infill panels are brick; rigid steel frames carry a timber roof. The exposed frame inside the church is painted white and the brick panels golden yellow. Exposed purlins are painted white and the boarding between light blue.

Centre (left): chapel at Arthur's Pass, Southern Alps (architect, Paul Pascoe). The design of this interdenominational chapel embodies a triple influence, the mountain hut (tent-like in form), the Maori meeting house (c.f. entrance and main porch) and an alpine chapel. Walls are a reinforced concrete core faced with alpine boulders and concrete blocks. The font is formed of three children's skis, crossed to hold the wood bowl.

Centre (right): church at Alexandra, Central Otago (architect, E. J. McCoy). A Roman Catholic church seating 350. The structure is of steel columns and portal frames; side walls are of concrete masonry with coloured glass squares 8 in. by 8 in. set into block courses and the end walls of reinforced concrete. A 12-in. skylight strip runs along the ridge of the roof above the nave to a larger skylight over the altar.

Church at Invercargill

Dental training school at Christchurch (architects, Warren and Mahoney); for about 100 nurses. Built in the grounds of an old mansion (which serves as a hostel) the school also contains a complete children's dental clinic. This occupies one wing and classrooms another, the two wings being joined by an administrative block at right-angles. The classroom and clinic wings, which require natural lighting, have fully glazed walls facing north, with shade canopies at two levels. They have light steel portal-frames and double walls of concrete blocks. Butterfly roofs rest on a central row of columns. The administrative block is timber-framed. Above: covered way leading to the entrance, with end of administrative block on right, and clinic on left. Below: interior of the clinic, which has 52 dental chairs.

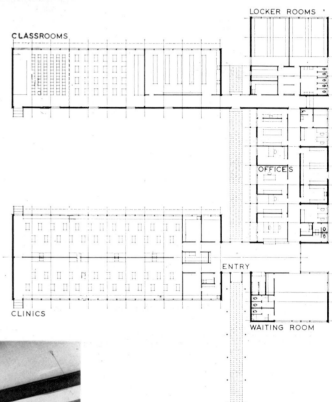

ground floor plan

Dental training school at Christchurch: north elevation of the clinic wing.

Memorial Hall, Napier (architects, Natusch and Sons),
a civic hall and beach pavilion, incorporating a war memorial
in the form of a roll of honour inscribed on granite slabs
around a pool, with fountain and flame of remembrance.
This lies behind the right-hand end of the curving tea-terrace,
and flanks the entrance to the hall. The screen-wall of the
terrace has load-bearing wooden mullions, concealing the
counterweights of the windows, and the hall has an exposed
reinforced concrete frame, with pre-stressed roof-beams.

Facing page: brewery at Palmerston North
(architect, Ronald J. McMillan). The
brewery tower is one element in a group of
new structures which are gradually replacing
an existing brewery. The influence of seismic
loading on the structure with respect to large
liquid masses, together with the combined
effect of soil pressures, were major
considerations in the design. Two elevations
are complete glass curtain-walls, one of which
hinges open for maintenance work; glazing
bars are white with centre mullions of
stainless steel; surrounding frames are
terracotta and the remainder of the exterior
is pale green.

Prototype School at Napier (architects, NZ Ministry of Works),
a 'cluster' layout, adaptable to differing sites and to expanding
communities, composed of a number of independent blocks,
each serving a related group of teaching functions. The
illustration shows the assembly-hall/administrative block.
Other blocks house library, arts and academic teaching,
or craft-rooms and laboratories, and the number of blocks can
be increased as the number of pupils increases and the
curriculum grows in complexity.

Parnell Baths, Judges Bay, Auckland (architect, T. K. Donner). Part of a comprehensive plan of redevelopment by the city council. It is bounded on the eastern and southern sides by a cliff which shelters it from the prevailing winds. The main building is a two storey reinforced concrete structure providing facilities for 3,000 people. Dual access is by pedestrian ramps on the east and west sides reached by a 6 ft. 6 in. wide cantilevered access-way which starts from a common point of entry on the north. The murals, executed in opaque glass chips set in white cement on asbestos cement panels, are by James Turkington, and are designed to harmonize with the painted floor of the pool.

Airport terminal building, Christchurch (architect, Paul Pascoe): planned with separate sections for internal and overseas airlines. A restaurant lies between them and the freight section occupies the southern end of the building. Airline offices occupy a first floor over the internal airways section, with the control tower alongside. Construction is reinforced concrete, with folded slab roof and steel girders used where large spans are required. Above: from the land side. This building was awarded the New Zealand Institute of Architects' Gold Medal for 1961.

New Zealand

Right: the main concourse at
Christchurch airport. The staircase
from the waiting lounge leads to a
balcony with bookstall, etc. from
which an open 'farewell balcony'
(right of picture) is reached. The
balcony also gives a view of the
Southern Alps. Internal colouring is
mostly grey with natural wood,
clear varnished, black railings and
strong colours used in the furnishings. Below: the ground floor plan.

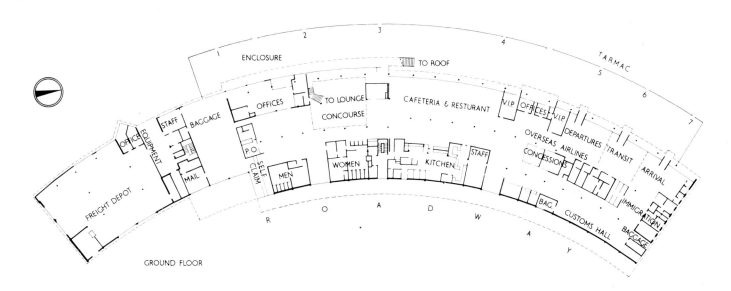

GROUND FLOOR

Hotel in the Southern Alps (architects, Hall and Mackenzie).
In 1957 the mountain hotel known as the Hermitage was burnt
down. It had to be rebuilt quickly and despite the difficult and remote
terrain and the exceptional rainfall (260 inches during the period
of the contract), it was completed within twenty-six weeks. The
construction is damp-proofed double concrete slabs for the ground
floors, timber framed walls and roofs; exterior sheathing is of oiled
sawn cedar weatherboards; interior, Gibraltar board and fibrous
plaster. Stone walls and fireplaces are random coursed split glacial
moraine boulders. There is an oil-fired low-pressure heating system.

TO DEFINE THE NATURE OF Canadian architecture is to embark upon the definition of a mirage. It flitters in the landscape. As you approach it, as you stretch out your hand to touch and open your mind to comprehend it, the phantom vanishes. In its place the landscape reappears, a landscape which has all the variety one would encounter travelling between Bordeaux and Vladivostok. Can one visualize clearly a Canadian architecture with such a kaleidoscopic background?

The country's history, its geographical position, north of the United States, west of Britain and France, and east of the Orient, its pattern of multi-racial settlements, its economic and social dependency are all factors contributing to a blurring of outlines, a conflict of motives, and indecision as to what is right for Canada, the whole of Canada. Nevertheless, in this architectural penumbra, certain clear statements are being made. The merging of these will perhaps result, over the years, in an architectural expression which can be defined as 'Canadian.' What are some of these architectural statements?

With a powerful country such as the United States sharing 4,000 miles of boundary, and being the only country with which Canada shares an active boundary, it is inevitable that the influence of this colossus should be quite considerable. This has been evident ever since the war of 1812–14 between the two countries. Since that war a growing friendship has linked them in many forms of joint enterprise and exchange of ideas. Economic rivalry and, eventually, domination and exploitation have not hampered this exchange. On the other hand, the many American-owned enterprises in Canada have brought very definite architectural influences. The vast amount of printed material, trade literature, architectural magazines and books or other cultural works which come to Canada from the USA, have made the Canadians conscious of developments in that country as they are conscious of developments in no other. Also, the good expressways which link Canada to the United States are crowded with sightseers. Canadians form the largest national group of visitors to the United States. It is therefore not surprising to find, since the middle of the last century, an increasing number of buildings the designs for which have either originated in the United States or have been derived from American examples. The work of Richardson in the Boston area had a great influence at the end of the nineteenth century and the beginning of this one, when many buildings throughout eastern Canada, and even some in the west, emulated a large-paned type of romantic Romanesque, amplified with turrets and bay-windows. Today, Skidmore, Owings and Merrill are exerting a comparable influence.

As to Canada's own architectural history, one period should be mentioned especially. This was the period of the great pioneering barons who were developing their financial and political empires. This was the Canadian Victorian era and it was a good reflection of the same era in the home country, England. Only, in Canada it gained a greater zest and vitality. It was an eclectic period, but also a creative one, when any building was considered as a historic challenge, resulting in more exaggeration, greater lustfulness. Unfortunately these buildings are impossible to live in today, and they are fast disappearing from Canadian cities to make way for blank-faced intimidated curtain-walled boxes, reflective of the current spiritual poverty.

At the height of Canada's expansion westward at the turn of the century, especially during the years immediately prior to World War I, immigration was encouraged, and up to over 400,000 people a year came to settle there. While the majority came from the British Isles, continuing the importation of British culture, great numbers came from other countries, especially from northern Europe and the Ukraine. Across the land, in every city and on many a farmstead, a bit of Europe was transplanted: an onion-shaped dome or cupola, a bit of Polish fretwork, a Dutch gable, Scandinavian reds and ochres and their flat trim-surrounds, Germanic precise window-rhythms, Swiss chalet balconies and Ukranian farm porches. Out of this melting pot, combined with the original French and subsequent British cultures, a native architecture is perhaps in the making. But the giant to the south is also a multi-nationality boiling pot of ideas, influences and traditions. So, again, it is natural that the architectural paths of these two countries should be similar.

On the far west coast, in British Columbia, particularly in its magnificently set major port-city of Vancouver, a somewhat more independent development has taken place. Predominantly British, this area has also long felt the influence of the Orient. It has been ready to accept ideas in the use of wood from Japan, in fretwork decoration from China and in modular and open planning from both. This region has led Canada in exploring new architectural ideas as it has in painting, and its contemporary houses and other buildings have a distinction which has induced the 'BC style' in eastern Canada. Some office buildings and numerous residences in the Vancouver area are as fine as can be found. The BC Electric Company's head-office building is considered by many critics to be the most gracefully handsome office building erected anywhere, a building which has a full integration of the work of artist and architect.

The years following the second World War have seen the emergence of a younger group of architects who are little different from young architects in any country. They revolted from eclectic and Victorian architecture. They became contemporary eclectics. Others tried desperately to be different and unique, but the curtain-wall and sheer façade, with little or no relief, gradually became insidiously pervading and the dominant trademark of modern architecture. But revolt is now setting in.

66

The country's largest firm, J. B. Parkin and Associates, which patterns itself after Skidmore, Owings and Merrill with a little more of Mies van der Rohe's influence, has moved towards a greater plasticity in the exterior treatment of its buildings, and greater formality in its plans. This firm's influence on architectural thinking is considerable. In a similar style, and with equal influence, Green, Blankstein, Russell and Associates of Winnipeg, Thompson, Berwick and Pratt of Vancouver, and Lebensold, Affleck, Desbarats, Dimikopoulos, Michaud and Sise, of Montreal, have been blanketing the country with competent, well-designed buildings. They are not as technically perfect and impressive as their American counterparts. They are, perhaps, softer in appearance, with a greater human content as a result of a lesser degree of industrial fabrication of their parts.

Besides and beyond these large firms are a number of small firms and individuals, too numerous to name, who are the conscience of the profession and who are primarily the products of the schools of architecture since the war. These architects are trying to bring back design dignity to the profession. Their designs are controlled and follow a simple order in the planning, in the structure and in the visual effect. Symbolism, significant form, is receiving more attention, as are some basic precepts: the articulation of the base, the body, the cover, and of the major components, structure, entrances and windows. There is a strong move away from the arid curtain-walls which may unfortunately cause its elimination from many logical uses. The move is not a purely negative one, as it emphasizes human reaction to the building: the need for man to find visual and emotional contact and pleasure as he experiences the building. This approach lays more stress on the aesthetic solution than on technical achievement, and herein lies the potential for a major difference between Canadian and American architecture.

In Canada there are five schools of architecture: in Montreal, McGill and the French Ecole des Beaux Arts; in Toronto, in Winnipeg and in Vancouver. They all follow the usual pattern of a five-year professional course following senior matriculation or first year of Arts and Science. The standard is high and comparable to the best schools in the United States. The youngest school, at the University of British Columbia, Vancouver, is, however, breaking rank. It will require at least three years of Arts and Science, or normally a Bachelor's degree in Arts or Science, prior to entry into a professional course having a minimum of three longer-than-usual academic years.

In conclusion, the North should be mentioned. This vast lake-studded frozen area of rock, tundra and scrub trees is offering tremendous industrial opportunities. Currently it is a vital part of the North American defence system. Modern science is invading this lonely primitive land. It may be that in solving the unique building problems of this area a truly Canadian form of architecture will emerge, re-shaping the modern-eclectic forms of the southern populated belt of the country.

The many trends of the country, a country of many national heritages and of many geographic regions, need a catalyst. That catalyst may come from the north but it will act differently in Canada's various regions, in the maritime Atlantic provinces, in French-Canadian Quebec, in industrial Ontario, in the flat spacious and rigorous Prairies and in the mild-weathered and scenic Pacific Coast area. A Canadian architecture is unlikely. A Canadian architectural contribution is much more of a possibility.

F. LASERRE

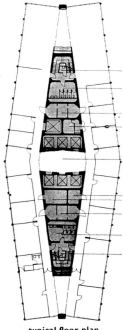

typical floor plan

Offices in Vancouver
(architects, Thompson,
Berwick and Pratt), for the
BC Electrical Board, who
already had a sub-station by
the same architects on part
of the same site, which had to
be fitted into the scheme. The
twenty four storey steel-
framed tower has a double-
tapering plan (above) in order
to secure the most compact
possible planning of the
service core and circulation
spaces, but all the office areas
are rectangular in plan
(except for the ones behind
the angles of the two main
façades) even at the end of
the block, thus producing the
re-entrants seen in the
illustration. The cladding is
of enamelled steel and
double-paned glass.

Left: night view of the twenty-four storey office tower at Vancouver, by Thompson, Berwick and Pratt, illustrated on the preceding page, showing how the newest architecture is beginning to dominate this fast-growing city.

Office block, Toronto (architect, James A. Murray), a straightforward curtain-wall design – no advertising is allowed in the largely residential area where it is sited – on a reinforced concrete frame. Unusually for such a building, the lower part is a club, with restaurant in the basement, and lounge bar on the ground floor. The staircase, illustrated above, is carried on a single spiral beam supported only at top and bottom.

Office block, Toronto (architects, Marani and Morris), for the Shell oil company, on the avenue linking the business centre of the city with the Ontario Parliament Buildings. The main, twelve-floor tower rises from a T-shaped ground floor whose arms, parallel with the street, conceal car-parking areas. Maximum flexibility of partitioning and services was a primary design consideration, while extension of the block upwards by adding more floors is also envisaged, when the service floor containing mechanical equipment at the top of the present tower would remain as an intermediate distribution floor. At the client's wish, extensive use has been made of native Canadian materials for finishes. The building is air-conditioned.

Parking garage, Dundas Square, Toronto (architects, John B. Parkin Associates), one of two such garages (see next page) built for the Toronto Parking Authority. Both are somewhat alike in plan, with parking accommodation disposed on either side of the lifting gear that raises the cars, and moves them horizontally to their allotted bays. Economic considerations, and an awkward triangular site at Dundas Square, called for ingenuity in securing a workable ratio of structure to cars accommodated, and the very small tolerances on levels permitted by the mechanical equipment made it necessary to carry the foundations of the concrete structure down some 48 feet to avoid differential settlement.

Another parking garage (see previous page) for the Toronto Parking Authority (architects, John B. Parkin Associates). The open parking decks – this garage has seven – are built of concrete, with simple parapets and rails. The cars are hoisted by lifts.

Below: City Hall, Edmonton, Alberta (architects, Dewar, Stevenson and Stanley), on a site between 99th and 100th Streets, whose lack of parallelism is echoed in the angles chosen for the 'lenticular' plan of the main office tower, and the splay, on plan, between the projecting council-chamber and the lower public block to the right.

City Hall, Ottawa (architects, Rother, Bland and Trudeau), seen from across the Rideau River.

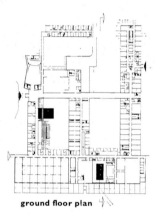

ground floor plan

Hospital and Rehabilitation Centre, Weston, Ontario (architects, Page and Steele), planned as far as possible on one level to facilitate the movement of the patients, who are workmen injured in industrial accidents. The plan encourages walking, which is part of the cure, and the occupational therapy wing has a deliberately industrial atmosphere. Structure is steel for the single-storey wings, and reinforced concrete for higher blocks for 500 patients.

Below: highway bridge, Belly River, Alberta (designers, Highways Department, Government of Alberta). It is built in four pre-stressed, pre-cast concrete spans, each of eighty feet.

Above: Railway Station, North Vancouver (architects, Hale Harrison Associates), handling the small but increasing passenger traffic on the Pacific Great Eastern since its link-up with Vancouver. The steel-frame building has thus been planned with expansion in mind. The concourse/ waiting area has a bar besides the usual facilities, and is glazed on the side towards the tracks to afford maximum view of railway operations.

Below: Arts Buildings, University of British Columbia, Vancouver (architects, Thompson, Berwick and Pratt), a complete collegiate unit, comprising a class-room block with open ground floor, giving on to a court flanked on one side by an office wing and on the other by a block of acting-studios and class-rooms; between this last and the main class-room block is a link unit with entrances, foyer and staircases.

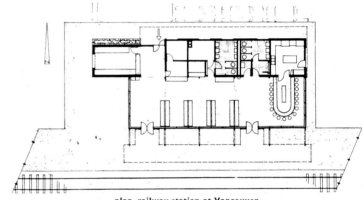

plan, railway station at Vancouver

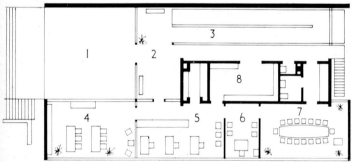

upper floor. 1, entrance foyer. 2, hall. 3, exhibition hall. 4, library. 5, general office. 6, secretary. 7, committee room. 8, storage.

Architects' headquarters, Toronto, for the Ontario Association of Architects (architects, John B. Parkin Associates). Planned on a 5 ft. module and entered on the upper floor (photograph above), owing to the slope of the site. The structure consists of a reinforced concrete raft with an exposed steel frame superstructure and brick panel walls. Below: north-west side from the ravine at the back of the building; inside the entrance, with sculpture by Jean Horne.

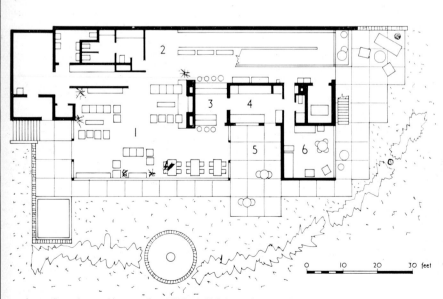

0   10   20   30 feet

lower floor. 1, assembly room. 2, exhibition hall. 3, bar and servery. 4, kitchen. 5, terrace. 6, caretaker.

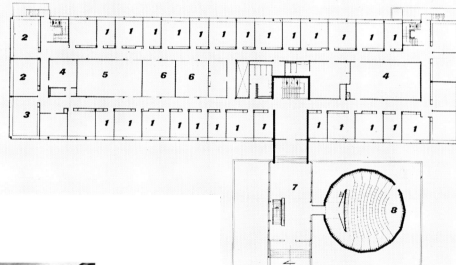

Offices at Sarnia, Ontario (architects, John B. Parkin Associates). A fully air-conditioned building for an oil company's engineers, analysts and technicians, situated near the company's refinery. In an attached wing is a circular assembly and lecture hall. The double corridor plan is repeated on the upper of the two office floors. A basement contains mechanical equipment, lunch-room and library. Construction is a welded steel frame with double-glazing and blue-grey porcelain enamelled panels between windows. Glazing beads are painted black and exposed steel white. Above: from the north, with entrance foyer on right, behind which is the circular hall. Left: from the south, showing the wall of the hall and entrance foyer beyond. The first floor plan, above, shows typical internal layout.

Shopping centre at Don Mills, Ontario (architects, John B. Parkin Associates). A group of small shops served by a pedestrian mall with planting and covered ways, part of the cluster of commercial and merchandising blocks on Lawrence Avenue East.

Banking Group, Don Mills (architects, John B. Parkin Associates), also on Lawrence Avenue East; a standardized architecture, related to that of the shopping centre, applied to a group of drive-in banks.

Federal Building, Don Mills (architects, John B. Parkin Associates): a square block not unlike a larger version of the banks illustrated above. The public hall for the post-office lies across the front of the building, set back from the columns carrying the roof (the other walls are flush with the structure) and one of its entrances is seen in this view.

Top: pharmaceutical factory and offices, Don Mills (architects, John B. Parkin Associates), a two-storey concrete framed block (the illustration shows the office entrance) with most of the offices at first-floor level and laboratories and work-spaces behind.

Above: housing at Don Mills (architects, James A. Murray and Henry Fliess); houses in blocks of four to six, each with its own garden. Houses are mainly of two types: a two-and-a-half floor type with a well-lighted basement, L-shaped living-dining room and three bedrooms above, and a split-level type with dining-room and kitchen at the entrance level and a sunken living-space and bedroom opening into the garden; other bedrooms and bathroom are up a half flight of stairs from the entrance level. The houses are grouped round common landscaped spaces, with car-parking out of view from the windows. They are in brick with shingled roofs and white painted door and window frames.

Canada

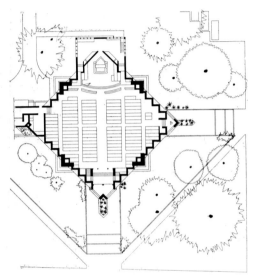

Church at Cartierville

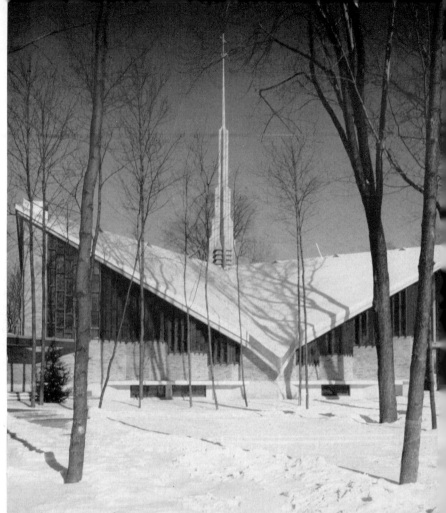

Above, right: Church of Notre Dame du Bel Amour, Cartierville, Montreal (architect, Roger D'Astous). Planned on the basis of a square whose diagonals are the ridges of a star-shaped vault. Eight triangular reinforced-concrete slabs rest on four piers. A continuous pleated strip of redwood window breaks up direct sunlight and helps to diffuse interior sound.

Right: Church at Toronto (architect, James A. Murray). Called the Yorkminster United Church, it is planned for a congregation of 500 with accommodation for social activities and Christian education. The approach from a main trans-Canada highway, with cloverleaf intersection which sets the scale, is by covered way alongside a sunken garden. The church hall and kitchen, which are at a lower level, are in reinforced concrete and the main floor is supported on steel beams. The superstructure is timber, with a frame of laminated members.

82

Racecourse, Etobicoke, Ontario (architect, Earle C. Morgan).
Designed with a view to future expansion. The present 1,100 horse
stalls can be increased to 1,400; parking for 16,000 cars can be increased
to 40,000; the stand which now seats 8,000 can be enlarged to seat
22,000. The grandstand has four seating levels and the clubhouse three,
the fourth level being the director's floor. The main betting ring floor is
at the top level of the apron, approximately 15 feet above grade at the
rear entrance side of the stand, thus freeing the grade level area for the
many ancillary requirements of a race track. The grandstand roof is in
the form of a huge truss supported at back and centre, and cantilevered
over the racecourse side.

Below: Construction Plant Depot, Burnaby, British Columbia (architects,
Thompson, Berwick and Pratt), a display and service centre for earth-
moving equipment, etc. Workshops, spare-parts store, and canteen are at
ground floor level, together with open-air display areas that are partly
sheltered by the steel-framed office floor, with its last eight bays
cantilevered above them.

Left and below: municipal offices, York Township, Ontario (architects, Shore and Moffat). Set back from a main avenue, and placed at an angle to give the best natural lighting and take advantage of a view up the valley to the north-west. The various departments occupy two floors and basement, with those requiring most contact with the public on the ground floor. The Police department is in a separate block, with a car-park between it and the main building. The offices are openly planned with the public space along the south side of the building separated from the working space only by counters or low partitions. On the first floor of the main building are the council chamber and committee rooms.

Alberta Jubilee Auditorium, Edmonton, Alberta (architect, Ronald Clarke). Erected, at the same time as a similar building at Calgary, to commemorate Alberta's fiftieth anniversary in 1955, the main auditorium has a seating capacity of over 1,500 people and is designed for orchestras, operas, and road shows as well as for presentations by local groups. In addition to the auditorium and its ancillary spaces, there are large promenades, club rooms, an exhibition area and a main social room with flanking smaller activity rooms. The structure is steel-frame with six three-hinged steel arches spanning the auditorium. The exterior is finished with pre-cast concrete panels and brick except for the main entrance which is faced with polished travertine.

Secondary school at Kitchener, Ontario (architects, Barnett and Rieder), a steel-frame building of more or less cruciform plan to house Eastwood Collegiate Institute. The long arm of the plan consists of a two-storey class-room block with a double gymnasium at its head, but at a lower level because of the fall of the site. The cross-arm contains the administrative block (visible in illustration) on one side, and the auditorium on the other.

Library, University of Manitoba, Winnipeg (architects, Green, Blankstein, Russell and Associates). The building, which includes a 75-seat theatre, exhibition space with a lounge opening off it and a small serving kitchen, is connected by a tunnel to the adjacent Arts Building to the south. Control of the library is split between two main desks, one on each of the ground and first floors; a book lift runs directly from these to the stack spaces. The structure is a reinforced concrete frame with hollow-core columns through which air is distributed to the stack areas. Exterior walls are of Manitoba Tyndall stone, random ashlar pattern; interior surfaces are oak and walnut panelling and plaster.

Right: lumber factory at Weston, Ontario (architects, Pentland and Baker). The site is on the outskirts of Toronto's metropolitan area. Besides the factory, warehouses and lumber yard, there is a general office building designed as two blocks linked by a main stairway. Timber and glass are the materials used throughout. A bay size of 20 ft. by 40 ft. was chosen as the one best suited to the 18-ft. maximum lumber length and the 4 by 4 palletted packages and 4 by 8 plywood sheet, the only exception being the millwork factory, where, because of the process, 80-foot spans were necessary. These support open trusses, glazed on the exterior face, on a 10-ft. module. The exterior walls of the factory and warehouse buildings are of 3-in. tongue-and-groove western Canadian cedar. Structural framing is glue-laminated beam and post. The office building is sealed and fully air-conditioned.

Above: hotel extension at Toronto (architects, Page and Steele), a wing added to the existing structure of the Park Plaza Hotel, and joined to it by a foyer and communicating public rooms. The first floor of the concrete column-and-slab structure has staff and reception rooms, the ground floor a dining room, lounge and rentable space.

Above, right: Seaway Hotel (architects, Elken and Becksted), at the west approach to Toronto, on made-ground between Lake Ontario and the railway. It has 111 rooms on four floors, all facing the lake with a corridor on the other side. At the east end is a two-storey block containing restaurant and convention and banqueting hall. It has a concrete frame with end walls of red brick.

Below: Festival Theatre, Stratford, Ontario (architects, Rounthwaite and Fairfield). The site falls 17 feet from south to north, and auditorium seating, stage and most service facilities are below ground level. The building is a 200-foot diameter circle in plan with a 40-foot foyer extending 160 feet along the south-west side. The arc of the audience area is 220 degrees and each member of the 2,192 audience has a view unobstructed by any vertical supports. This is achieved by a 'parasol' roof of thirty-four steel beams carried by a concrete ring resting on the inner columns of the promenade. The beams are locked together at the top, and stiffened by struts at two-thirds span, while the concrete ring is buttressed by the folded slabs of the promenade roof.

Top: flats at Calgary, Alberta (architect, Peter Caspary). The six separate buildings (set in fourteen acres of gardens) comprise eight basic types of flat, from 2 to 4½ rooms, though two of the types can be combined to produce 7 and 8 room flats. All flats above ground floor have balconies running their entire length with views over the Rocky Mountains. The scheme includes a neighbourhood store. All windows are double-glazed and there are automatic laundries for the use of the tenants.

Above: flats at Toronto (architect, Peter Caspary). Situated in the centre of Toronto, on a four-acre site, there are three fifteen-storey blocks with five different types of flat, ranging in size from the bed-sitting room to the two-bedroom flat. Each, above ground, has a full-width balcony. The structure is of reinforced concrete; the main entrance hall, which has murals in Italian mosaic, has floors of green, and walls of yellow, marble. All windows are wood-frame, double-glazed, screened and have bamboo curtains provided inside. There are three underground garages and a surface park, providing facilities for 550 cars.

Flats at Toronto (architects, Page and Steele), at 500 Avenue Road. The reinforced concrete structure accommodates eight large apartments on each of twelve main floors, with car-parking in the basement to clear all the rest of the plot for landscaping.

Flats at Toronto (architect, James A. Murray). The building is raised half a floor above ground to provide a car park beneath. The structure is of reinforced concrete, and there are eighty flats in the building which is on a high-density city site.

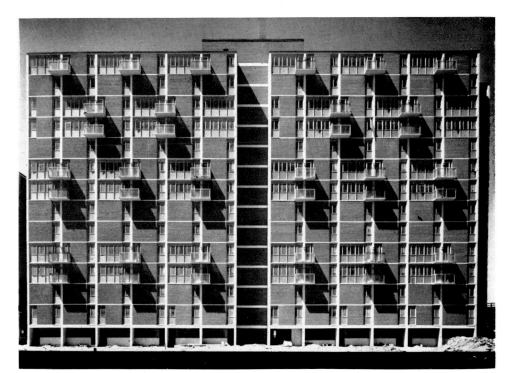

Re-development housing at Toronto (architects, Page and Steele), at Regents Park South, a mixed scheme of terrace-houses and high-rise blocks such as that shown here. The tall blocks have, effectively, cross-wall construction and skip-level sections, with maisonettes opening up and down from the access corridors, as the elevation clearly shows.

Flats at Toronto (architects, Page and Steele), at 561 Avenue Road, an earlier part of the development illustrated at the top of the facing page. The fourteen-storey reinforced-concrete structure has six flats per floor, each with a balcony, basement car-parking, ground floor lounge and dining room. On some floors the standard flat-plans have been varied to tenants' requirements.

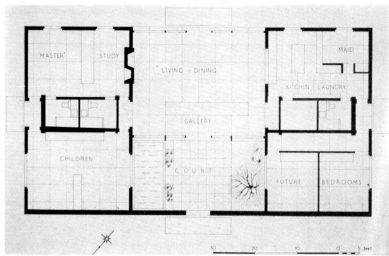

House at Todmorden, near Toronto (architects, John B. Parkin Associates), for Mr Parkin's own occupation. Slightly raised on an earth platform, it is approached diagonally so that the north-east and north-west fronts (above) are seen obliquely. It is planned on a four-foot module round an open entrance courtyard. Materials include white bricks spotted in black, whitish marble terrazzo and oiled walnut. The exposed pre-cast pre-stressed concrete flat roof can be flooded for coolness. The house is on one floor, has under-floor warm-air heating and is fully air-conditioned and double-glazed. Below: from the east.

House at Hamilton, Ontario (architect, Jerome Markson). Construction: steel box columns and exposed steel beams with walls of American beige brick. Floors: white terrazzo or broadloom on a concrete slab supported on open welded steel joists. Roof: wood deck on open-welded steel joists. Panelling and trim: walnut. Windows: fir-framed, double-glazed.

House at Toronto (architect, Irving Grossman), in a newly developed suburb. The entrance is through a small sheltered court with a pool and fountain. Most rooms face the back, where there is a view of a wooded ravine. There are no windows at the sides. The sloping site allows the lower level to open on to a terrace, which is sheltered by the living room balcony above. The cross-section, with secondary bedrooms on an upper floor, arose from local by-laws requiring two storeys for part of the house. Construction is load-bearing brick with stone external walls and timber floors and roofs.

The end of a row of cedar-finished houses in the housing scheme at Stanrock Uranium Mine, Elliot Lake, Ontario, which is illustrated on the facing page.

Housing at Stanrock Uranium Mine, Elliot Lake, Ontario
(architect, Jerome Markson). Elliot Lake had a population
of 25,000 only three years after its development began.
The houses had to be economical to build and operate.
The foundations and retaining walls are of poured concrete,
finished with white rendered concrete and cedar siding;
the asbestos-cement on the two-storey row houses is painted
in different shades of brown. The double-glazed fixed and
sliding windows are in pine frames.

House at Ottawa (architect, C. B. Greenberg), a three-bedroom timber house on a wooded site, the bedrooms lying across the house behind the blank wall to the left in the illustration. The rest of the house, which is glazed almost down to the floor on both sides, consists chiefly of a very large living room containing a kitchen area backed up on a bathroom/toilet core which separates it from the bedrooms.

House at Vancouver, British Columbia (architects, Leon G. Dirssar and H. Peter Oberlander). Standing in a large meadow facing south across the Straits of Georgia, the house is virtually a box on a table, the first floor being a conventional wooden frame structure supported on wooden posts and beams. All the living accommodation is on the first floor and a balcony across the south living room wall leads down to a sitting-out area which, with the rest of the ground floor, provides a sheltered space for open-air activities in a climate which, though mild, is often very rainy. Windows and doors are aluminium-frame and slide horizontally. Right: the staircase.

Part 2. The Tropical Territories

Part 2. The Tropical Territories: Introduction

'WHERE WINTER NEVER COMES' aptly describes the countries whose architecture is reviewed in the second part of this book. Here man builds to shelter from the heat of the sun; protection against cold is secondary, or unnecessary. But within the generality of warm climates, there is marked diversity. To divide them, as is often done, into warm-humid and hot-dry is sometimes convenient; but it hides features of significance and, on occasions, can be misleading. For example, Aden is hot and arid, yet being on the coast its air is humid.

Next to their concern with building to give shelter from the sun rather than from winter cold, the architects whose work is described here share in common the fact that they are working in the less industrially developed areas of the world, in countries which have recently emerged into nationhood or are still on that road. In some places – Hong Kong and Singapore, for example – building industries not very different from those of older Commonwealth countries are to be found. But in the Borneo territories, in some of the smaller West Indies and Pacific Islands, and outside the bigger towns in Africa, for a building of any size the contractor is likely to come from a distance, possibly from overseas, bringing with him materials and skilled labour.

A few of the places included here have had links with Britain for two hundred and fifty years or more. Barbados, for example, was first settled in 1627. The earliest recorded English trading voyage to the Gold Coast – now part of Ghana – was made by Thomas Windham in 1553. In others, the links are little more than half a century old. The British administration in the now independent north of Nigeria dates from 1900; that of the East African Protectorate – now Kenya – from 1895.

Mostly the predominant influence is that of Great Britain merging with local cultures – which are sometimes well developed, as in the lands of the Yoruba and Hausa peoples of Nigeria; sometimes not, as in most of East and Central Africa. But it is not always so. In the Far East, the cultural traditions of China and the Malay peoples are strong local influences. Not only have Moslem and Hindu cultures merged with that of Britain to form the heritage of the republics of India and Pakistan, but people from the Indian sub-culture have brought their influences with them to places as far apart as Fiji, British Guiana, Mauritius and Trinidad. There are some places where European influences other than British are to be seen. One such is Mauritius, once a thriving French settlement; in the eighteenth century its capital was then the second largest town in the whole of the southern hemisphere.

The countries and city states included in this part fall into seven more or less distinct groups. The West Indies, with British Guiana and Honduras (population over $3\frac{1}{2}$ million) mostly of Euro-African descent but with a significant East Indian minority. West Africa, composed largely of the independent countries of Nigeria (over 35 million inhabitants), Ghana (over $4\frac{1}{2}$ million) and Sierra Leone, now also independent, with over 2 million – all but a few thousand of these people are African. East Africa – over 21 million people, mostly African but with economically important groups from Europe and India. The Rhodesias, with Nyasaland – nearly 8 million, all but a quarter-million African. The great countries of south Asia – Ceylon, India and Pakistan – with a teeming population now nearing 500 million. The countries and cities of the Far East – independent Malaya with its $6\frac{1}{2}$ million (just over half being Malays), Singapore and Hong Kong, city states of $1\frac{1}{2}$ and 3 million respectively, largely Chinese; and the much less developed territories of Borneo. And, lastly, a group of smaller territories – mostly islands – who share in common British administration.

The West Indies enjoy an architectural tradition centuries old. Its origin was mainly Georgian England, though the work was more in the manner of a plain West Country builder than in the sophisticated style of a London architect. In the smaller islands, a simple classical manner lingered on until almost this century, but gradually fell victim to neglect, incompetence, and mediocrity. Gardner-Medwin, and the young architects who followed him in the late 1940's, revived the spirit of the earlier period – simplicity, and a sense of space and openness. Despite distractions from North America, these earlier traditions are still an important influence on the trade-wind architecture of the West Indies.

In contrast, the architectural traditions of eighteenth-century Britain in India perished some time before the ending of the British Raj. For a time they were continued in increasingly debased form by military engineer-architects and their civilian successors, doing the ordinary run of government work. But buildings of importance were reserved for the eminent London architect who brought, or sent out, little but the confusions of Victorian England and ignored or despised things Indian. Thus grew the chasm between civil engineer and architect which, in India and Pakistan, has yet to be bridged securely. With the building of New Delhi, the adoption of an Imperial, classical architecture as a deliberate attempt to reflect in building the concept of the mission of the Empire, reached its apogee. To this day, only occasionally have Indian architects mastered the conflicting influences of foreign manners, local vernaculars, the spirit of Imperial Delhi, and Public Works Department rules and procedures.

Being outposts, Malaya and Hong Kong were more fortunate. The early works of English classical tradition, though more substantial and later in date, had much in common with those in the West Indies. Though the Imperial style has left its mark on Singapore, there is nothing of the ugly confusion of

Bombay or Calcutta. Architecture has long been acknowledged as a profession. Compared with India or even Ceylon, by the time of its independence Malaya had come to understand better the role of the architect in public building. As in Hong Kong, it now follows more the organization of a good English country office than that of the usual government building department in an Asian country.

Many of the buildings illustrated have been designed by architects from Great Britain, a number of whom, especially in West Africa, have set up offices locally. Some are the work of architects from the United Kingdom or one of the other older Commonwealth countries who have joined the local public service. Quite a number of the buildings, particularly in the West Indies, Rhodesia and the Asian countries, are designed by architects who are locally born or who have made a home in the country where they are now working. Most have been trained in Britain, Australia or another of the older Commonwealth countries, though India, for example, has for many years had its own school of architecture. During the 1950's, architectural schools have been established in East and West Africa, Hong Kong, Malaya and Singapore. Before long, their students will play an important part in developing local architectural traditions.

Again the 1950's have seen the establishment of local industries for making building materials. Portland cement is now manufactured in the West Indies, West and East Africa, Malaya and Hong Kong, as well as in Ceylon, India and Pakistan; and it is concrete rather than brick which is the mass material of construction in almost all the buildings described. In a number of the countries, local building stone and timber are used as a contrast to concrete work. But many of the sheet materials, finishes, fittings and equipment are imported from Europe, North America or, in the case of the Far East, from Japan.

To return to the matter of climate and its effects on design: in no two places is it quite the same; invariably one at least of the determining influences – such as latitude, height above sea-level, nearness to the sea or other large body of water and to hills or mountains, wetness of the ground and the nature of its vegetation – is different. Moreover, man changes the climate by cutting down forests, draining swamps, damming rivers and polluting the air. Very local differences are likewise caused by buildings, roads, and open spaces. Generally, it is warmer and drier in the centre of a town; breezes blow less strongly; and the sun, because of dust and smoke, shines less fiercely. Descriptions of climates are usually based on meteorological observations made at the local airfield or on an open site out of town. In tropical countries conditions in towns are likely to be more trying to man and less so to his work.

Whatever the climate, in the countries described in this part, except in the highlands and at or beyond the tropics in the winter season, shade from the heat of the sun is of first importance. Anyone entering a 'wide vision' car which has been standing closed in the hot sun becomes aware of the drawback of lack of shade. In a cold climate, we welcome the fact that ordinary glass discriminates between radiation of different wavelengths, letting in the sun's heat and light, yet returning to the sky and surroundings only a small part of the room's heat, which is radiated at low temperature. But, in a warm climate, there is little to be said for unshaded glass – except for making solar heaters.

Shading devices, as many of the illustrations which follow show, have become a symbol of tropical architecture. Except in the early morning in the cool season, direct sunlight through windows and doors has to be avoided, especially if openings are glazed, or the building air-conditioned. North- and south-facing openings can be shaded with horizontal canopies, which also permit windows to be kept open when it is raining – most important where it is warm and humid. West- and east-facing openings, on the other hand, require vertical shades which, if fixed, screen the view and cut down the daylight. For this reason, many of the buildings are sited with their longer axis running east and west.

When it is warm, and especially when it is also humid, movement of air across the skin makes one feel cool. In a place like Singapore, where it never gets very hot or very cold, a building not air-conditioned is best made as open as possible to offer least resistance to light winds. Shade against the sun and protection against rain, sky-glare and, probably, insects, intruders and the gaze of neighbours, usually makes screening necessary, though it cuts down the breeze. These screens, again, are a feature of much of the work shown. Mechanical fans are used to move the air when the wind drops. Especially during the late afternoon and evening, abundant fresh air is needed to keep a building cool. The heat of the sun gained during the day by the structure has by then reached the interior. Lightness is an advantage. The breeze is likely to drop. Any exchange of air between indoors and outdoors is predominantly by stack effect. So, louvred vents placed high up in the wall are advantageous or, better, two-storey buildings with open staircases. Away from the ground the wind is stronger, so upper floors of high buildings are cooler.

In the trade-wind belts farther from the equator the wind blows persistently for most of the year, at least on windward coasts. If a building is too open, papers and furnishings are blown about; yet, for comfort, some air movement is needed. By facing the building away from the wind and making the leeward side the more open, air is drawn through the building. Screens also break the force of the wind. In places high above sea-level, like Nairobi, and in the winter season at and beyond the tropics, as in Hong Kong, a permanently open building is too well ventilated and will be too cool at times. Ventilation must be controlled. In places where it may be hot and dry one season of the year, like north India and Northern Nigeria, it should also be possible to close ventilators and windows to exclude the dust and the heat of the day. But in such places abundant fresh air is needed to cool the building down rapidly after sunset. Mechanical ventilation helps to draw in the cooler night air. During the dry season in such climates 'desert coolers' – fans which draw the outside air through some form of wetted screen – cool, but also make more humid the air indoors.

In warm climates, the dominant thermal problem is to check the passage of the sun's heat into a building. The air temperature tends to rise in occupied buildings and, except at high altitudes and in the winter season at and beyond the tropics, the ambient temperature is above the comfort zone by day. It is necessary to limit the rise to a small and, if possible, negligible value. At night the temperature outdoors is lower. In an equatorial climate, where people are particularly sensitive to changes in temperature, indoor temperatures up to about 5° F. above that outdoors are often found desirable for comfort. During the hot season in places at and beyond the tropics, however, a building may have been so heated by the sun during the day, that as large a fall in temperature after dark as possible is welcome; even then it may be uncomfortably hot indoors after dark, especially in a heavyweight building. Under such conditions people sleep on rooftops or elsewhere out of doors, and screened places are needed for this.

The first line of defence against solar-heat gain is shade, particularly for the roof, windows and west-facing walls. Subject to practical considerations, sun-shades are made light in weight so that they can cool down rapidly after dark; their design must avoid both trapping the heated air and, in a humid climate, encouraging mould growth. Most of the buildings shown have, therefore, white or near-white façades; though the most successful have also taken care to avoid being excessively bright to the view from inside.

Whether the main structure is well insulated or not, is light or heavy in weight – or, more accurately, has a low or high thermal capacity – depends on whether its surface is sunlit or shaded, whether the daily range in temperature is large or small, whether day-time or night-time use is the more important, and whether the building is naturally ventilated or air-conditioned. In a warm, humid climate, where the air temperature in shade varies by less than, say, 10° F. in the twenty-four hours, it will be a little warmer and a little drier at night indoors than in the open. Compared with a lightweight building, a heavyweight structure will be somewhat cooler until afternoon but warmer in the evening. But weight is of less importance than ample air movement. In a hot, dry climate, however, the daily range of temperature may be 25–30° F., and the damping effect of weight should not be ignored. A heavyweight structure, with windows closed during the day, is markedly cooler until nightfall; but it responds much more slowly to the drop in outdoor air temperature after dark.

Shading and thermal insulation reduce the amount of heat passing into a building. Thermal capacity retards its passage, which means that it can be cooler indoors during the day but, as a result, will be hotter at night. Neither can make a building cooler than shade-temperature over the twenty-four hours. (Normal buildings are likely to be 3–5° F. warmer than the outdoor air over this whole period.) Air movement makes one feel cooler but, with one exception, cannot cool the air below shade-temperature. The exception is in dry climates where the air temperature can be lowered by evaporative cooling: i.e. passing the air through a moist screen – the 'desert cooler' mentioned earlier. None of these devices can dry the air; evaporative coolers make it moister, which is unimportant in a dry climate. To cool a building over twenty-four hours, refrigeration is necessary, filtered air being drawn by fan over a chilled coil. Part of the moisture in the air is removed as condensate, the disposal of which can be a problem where unit room-coolers are used. To cool a building costs possibly three times as much as to heat it volume for volume. In equatorial climates the system will be operating throughout the year. Air-conditioning is, therefore, expensive. Moreover it creates a barrier between the air-conditioned man and his surrounding which is rarely desirable. Some of the buildings illustrated here are air-conditioned – particularly the offices in the centre of towns. But in most tropical countries it is likely that air-conditioning will continue to be the exception rather than the rule – at least in its present form. (It is questionable whether the present basis of air-conditioning design, particularly for equatorial climates, is correct. Too much attention is probably being given to lowering the temperature of the air, and not enough to drying it and ensuring that there is a good flow of air throughout the space being treated.)

In tropical areas, it might be thought that artificial cooling would free architects from the need to design specially for the local climate. But this is not so. If the system is to be reasonably efficient, the cooling load must be kept down by shading and a high standard of insulation and, in a humid climate, by a vapour barrier. Kitchens and similar producers of heat and moisture within the conditioned space have to be treated at source; building volume kept to a minimum, and plans kept compact. Open areas rising two-storeys high – advantageous for naturally ventilated buildings in equatorial climates – have to be avoided in air-conditioned buildings; the hot air rises to the upper floor, making it uncomfortable when the building becomes crowded.

Equatorial climates produce abundant vegetation. Grassed areas can be established in a matter of months. Planting can be one of the most rewarding tasks, but to keep gardens under control calls for continuous work. Trees, many of which have coloured flowers, grow fast. Rightly sited, they give shade and protection from sky glare. The most successful of the buildings shown are those which make use of the broken topography of their sites and local vegetation, relating open interiors to the surrounding garden. In drier climates near the tropics, at least during the dry season, gardens often have to be irrigated. Water is expensive, and areas of grass and plants usually have to be kept small. Screen walls confine the prospect; they also serve to control blown sand and dust. Bare ground needs to be hard-surfaced. Small areas of water give a sense of refreshing coolness. The illustrations of buildings in Ceylon and at Chandigarh show the contrast between the plant life of an equatorial climate and the aridity of north India.

To conclude: as the buildings illustrated on the pages that follow show, the principle elements of tropical architecture are all related to climate. They are:

The open air. In most climates, some time in the year, in daytime or at night, it is most pleasant to be in the open air – hence the importance of screens and the right use of grass, flowers, shrubs, and trees.

Screened and shaded but open space. Verandahs, porches, well-ventilated rooms, and the like, open to natural breezes but protected from direct sunlight, the rain, and, possibly, the bright light of clouds and other sunlit surfaces. In equatorial climates, the whole building is formed of such spaces.

Enclosed space, naturally cooled. In climates where, in summer, it becomes very hot during the day, one needs to close-up rooms completely against the heat, glare and dust of the world outside; fans are needed to keep the air within this space moving, for comfort. After dark, it should be abundantly ventilated and thus cooled.

Enclosed space, mechanically cooled. A retreat, cut-off from all contact with the world outside – from noise, dust, insects, heat, glare (with louvred blinds), and other men.

G. A. ATKINSON

West Africa

WHAT WE CALL WEST AFRICA is a long strip of land lying between the South Sahara and the South Atlantic Ocean, comprising the one-time colonies and dependencies of Britain, France and Portugal. It is a fringe of rain forest that tapers off northward and westward. Until the last war it was a place known chiefly to traders, missionaries and the small number of officials that administered it. Its emergence into the full current of world affairs, and of its component countries into independence, is an effect of accelerated communication, due largely to war. Even before the end of the war Parliament had voted £200 millions under the Colonial Development and Welfare Act, enabling the earliest start to be made on the education, in the widest sense of the word, of peoples who had hitherto been entirely subservient to the primary producing needs of dependent colonies.

This defines the political attitude of Great Britain towards these countries. It also indicates their emotional response to the situation and explains the rapid technical advances made: not rapid enough for the peoples concerned, but appearing too rapid to many an outside observer.

In 1944, when Jane Drew and I started planning and building in West Africa, little of this was apparent. India was still a dominion, and the Empire was virtually intact. Nevertheless, the change was in the air, and my own attitude to our work was that it was an instrument of introduction to European life and thought. For good or ill a decision had been made by both parties to the affair. There was no question of turning back on any tracks. It was a matter of making the most of the situation given. It was a matter, more precisely, of planning tropical towns for modern life in the fullest sense of the term; of building schools and universities for an unrestricted range of education; and, in all this, of foreseeing an advance on the widest technological front. At the outset the impediments to carrying out a large programme of buildings were formidable. The building industry consisted of a few under-organized and badly equipped firms using illiterate but not unintelligent local workmen. It needed, and without question accepted, the regulating machinery current in more highly developed countries – a detailed building agreement, cost accountancy as understood by quantity surveyors, payment by measurement on accurate and detailed architects' and engineers' drawings, expert supervision.

The main interest for architects lies elsewhere, and concerns the application of CIAM principles and methods to comprehensive problems of tropical architecture and planning. It is on that score that the achievement in West Africa will be measured. It concerned first the needs of the people, which in the first few years came to us all in terms of education, and secondly it concerned climate, which I have come more and more to respect as a determining factor of architecture, because it has already determined so much else, from agriculture to the habits, customs and, finally, religions of peoples who live dependent upon it. When we study climate we are seeking an accommodation with nature; we are searching for the particular form from amid the general order of things, in hopes of fashioning what will be uniquely applicable to conditions as we see them. In doing so we are creating a regional character answerable to local needs, a dialect of internationalism.

The climate of the populous areas of West Africa is intensely tropical – hot, humid, rainy and insect-ridden, with fast growing vegetation, and the critical factor is humidity measured in terms of its effect on body heat-loss; or, put another way, on the cooling effect on the skin of moving air. To meet this condition buildings must generally be no more than one room thick and their construction must offer the minimum of obstruction to the passage of air. They must also be shaded from sun and protected from driving rain, and the quality of the moving air must be enhanced by the presence of vegetation. There are many other considerations, among the first of which is the necessity for orientation to keep sun off walls, to turn away from storms and – most important – to face into the breeze. Most of these conditions can be evaded by using air-conditioning, but without absolving the architect from his pre-occupation with climate, since the expense of air-conditioning makes it most sensitive to heat gains within the envelope, varying as they do with the daily passage of the sun across the building. The conditioning system already suffers from the costly necessity of extracting humidity by refrigeration, and can afford no further overload whatsoever.

So, therefore, climate presses from all directions, and few architects in any of their works have successfully dealt with them all. But they have developed a common attitude to the obsessing problem. The solutions in terms of building have changed enormously over fifteen years. The predominant building material of West Africa was, and perhaps still is, mud, which under the conditions of tribal life and economics, with its perpetual renewal through communal effort, was entirely appropriate. Under a system of cash-economy it becomes immediately expensive, no matter how low its original capital cost. This is one of the deplorable effects of the division of labour; one among many. The dominance of maintenance faces us also with our enemies the insects. Tribalism could tolerate them and mend and make do, but we must fight the termite and ant as we fight the anopheles mosquito, must resist fungus and corrosion and call on our armoury of scientific and industrial weapons in an attempt to outwear time. This explains why we jumped to reinforced concrete at the first moment possible, reducing everywhere the timber content of building and denying access to flying insect hordes. If, as in our library in Ibadan, Nigeria, an interior free from insects and a fabric offering no nourishment for termites can be created at low cost, a victory over circumstances has been registered. To make an air-conditioned library, as originally intended, has been shown to be beyond the reasonable means of such a university.

This rapid survey of the forces bearing on the evolution of architecture in West Africa stresses the simpler responses to them because these are the most important. The present building programme tends to obscure them because it is so much concerned with the building of the capital centres with their luxury hotels, large governmental and commercial buildings and the like. This work had to be done, but beyond it lies the immense task of raising the standards of life in low-income countries outside the showy capital cities; and for this is required first and foremost a housing and town-planning policy with a status equal to its first-class importance. If any West African Minister should read this article I would urge upon him the necessity of making town-planning a major instrument of government, with powers over land-use and with, as nearly as possible, a benevolent landlord's view of his responsibility. Just as architecture must deal with the conditions of climate and society in evolving a style suited to tropical Africa, so must town-planning study the peculiar needs of the region and plan accordingly. The evanescent nature of so much of the existing towns and villages makes it possible to replan at less expense than elsewhere in the world, although the major problems of industrialism and traffic congestion will be similar.

African life needs a different pattern, of different houses, than elsewhere. Its needs are peculiar and unique. They have been studied in detail by anthropologists and others, but unless the status of town-planning is improved and responsible researches undertaken rapidly, all this will go by default and towns will be built, or grow congested, with no directing impulse arising from knowledge of the conditions. Cheap housing, as we found in India, is of all architecture the most difficult to create, and even so cannot be considered apart from town-planning. What is important is not the individual unit but the life-cycle of which it is a part. I am not suggesting that town-planning is not being used. There is evidence of serious planning in many centres. The point I make is that, at the rate of development in West Africa, it should be given a still greater importance and the means of dealing with existing property, because of the incalculable benefits it will confer upon the changing lives of the people.

Much of the work shown in this section comes from the offices of expatriates like myself whom accident or good fortune brought to West Africa. We are, of course, part of the architectural history of the region and deeply involved with its evolution. But the next stage is being rehearsed in schools of architecture all over Britain, and in those now established at the Kumasi and the Zaria Colleges of Technology, which move rapidly towards recognition by the RIBA as centres of examination as well as teaching. It is quite some years since Mr T. S. Clark joined our Town-planning Office in Accra as its first West African representative, and went on from there to be the chief executive architect of the Tema Town Corporation. He was the first president of the

Ghana Society of Architects, now a chapter of the RIBA overseas. And in a recent visit to Accra, I saw large and splendid new government office buildings rising, pointing to the eventual condition in which West African architecture will be as West African as its people, but no longer isolated.

The greater part of the buildings shown in this section are in the more rapidly developing south. But in Nigeria, Ghana and Sierra Leone there are also areas in which the rain forest is thinning out to orchard bush and scrub, and humidity is evaporating towards the typical hot-dry tropic of the semi-desert. These regions are inhabited by people of Muslim faith, and in Nigeria they compose the majority of the total population of the country, but spread thinly over a vast area. For these people an entirely different architecture is needed, both because of the climate, which is critically hot with hot dust-laden winds, and also because of the social religious observances of the people. It is an architecture of shade and enclosure that sets a high value on water, which is as hard to find there as it is plentiful in the south. In the north, as well as in the south, the transformation of the West African countries into secular states on Western lines continues, imposing upon architects the great responsibility not only of providing buildings that will remain workable long into the future, but of investing them with a character emotionally in tune with the varied and dramatic circumstances of their time.

E. MAXWELL FRY

Ghana

Junior staff quarters, Government House, Accra (architect, J. G. Halstead, chief architect, Public Works Department; assistants in charge, D. A. Barratt and W. J. Clarke). They are sited near the seventeenth-century Danish castle which is now the official residence of the Prime Minister of Ghana. Right: an aerial view of three blocks of houses, planned round a square. Below: from outside the square. See also the next page.

Junior staff quarters, Government House, Accra (architect, J. G. Halstead, chief architect, Public Works Department). See also the preceding page. Twenty-four self-contained dwellings occupy a one-and-a-half acre site adjoining the grounds of the old Danish castle, the architectural character of which is to some extent echoed in the style of the dwellings, These are planned in three blocks, surrounding the centre of the site where there were outcrops of rock. The fourth side of the square is occupied by a laundry and drying-yard. The dwellings look inwards to the square, which provides a safe playing space for children. Each block (see plan) consists of units of three dwellings – two ground-floor, one first-floor – which are only one-room thick to provide cross-ventilation. Each dwelling has a private courtyard for open-air living and sleeping. Load-bearing walls are of rendered concrete blocks. Floors are reinforced concrete, roofs are timber, tiled, and windows and doors also timber. Below: the upper stories of several houses, with their enclosed service yards.

typical ground and first floor plans, junior staff quarters, Government House, Accra

1, banking hall.
2, manager's flat.
3, public car park.
4, manager's car park.
5, guards' quarters.
6, service yard.
7, warehouses and garages.

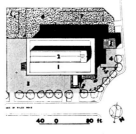

site plan, bank at Takoradi

Bank at Takoradi (architects, Drake and Lasdun). A large banking hall, shared by the Ghana Commercial Bank and the Bank of Ghana Currency Agency, is divided by light aluminium screens. Each user has a separate entrance, but they share strongrooms, staff-rooms, etc., which are at a lower level. A manager's flat is at roof level. Sun is excluded by the roof overhang and the projecting wall-fins. These, and the balcony, are faced with travertine. The base is faced with local stone. The main structure is concrete, the roof having a double skin for insulation. Windows are aluminium.

Hotel at Accra (architects, Kenneth Scott Associates): extensions to the existing Avenida Hotel, consisting of four-storey bedroom block (shown in photograph), restaurant and bar. The bedroom block has fourteen air-conditioned rooms, each with a bathroom. The structure is reinforced concrete with external walls and partitions of concrete blocks, rendered. Roofs are timber with wood-wool decking and felt. Staircases are cast-iron, helical type. Floors are terrazzo, and windows of aluminium, sliding horizontally, with Venetian blinds.

Dormitory block, Mfantsipim School, Cape Coast (architect, Kenneth H. Holgate): one of a group of three buildings (the others still under construction) providing dormitory space for 200 students, together with common-rooms, etc., for this Methodist church school. Construction is reinforced concrete frame with concrete block infill, rendered with cement and sand. Panels under windows are additionally rendered in colour, a pattern being made by the use of a plywood template. Roofing is asbestos. Doors, windows and all exposed woodwork are oiled mahogany.

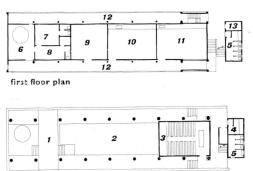

first floor plan

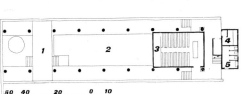

key
1, roadway.
2, garden.
3, lecture theatre.
4, dark room.
5, lavatories.
6, entrance hall.
7, headmaster.
8, secretary.
9, library.
10, studio.
11, gallery and store.
12, open balcony.
13, store.

50 40 20   0 10

ground floor plan: school of architecture, Kumasi

School of Architecture at Kumasi (architect, Charles I. Hobbis): the first section of a two-phase programme for the school of architecture, town planning and building, at Kumasi College of Technology. There is a partly open ground floor (see plans, right). On the second floor are three more studios and an exhibition hall; on the top floor one large classroom. The structure is reinforced concrete with walls of pre-cast blocks or local stone and aluminium roof.

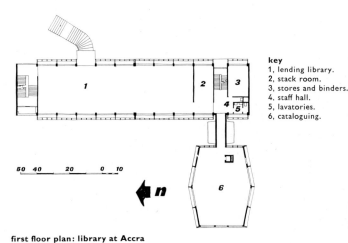

key
1, lending library.
2, stack room.
3, stores and binders.
4, staff hall.
5, lavatories.
6, cataloguing.

50 40 20   0 10

first floor plan: library at Accra

Library at Accra (architects, Nickson and Borys): a three-storey building in the centre of Accra near the classical-style Supreme Court. The ground floor is partly open, with parking area and services; on the first floor (see plan right) is the lending library and on the second the reference library. Stackrooms are behind. The brise-soleil, of pre-cast concrete units, faces the low morning and evening sun.

Above: Sports Stadium at Kumasi (architects, Kenneth Scott Associates). Part of a sports arena containing fields, running and cycle tracks, open terraces for 24,000 spectators and an office and committee building. This grandstand, seating 1,500, has changing rooms, dormitories and stores beneath it. It is of reinforced concrete with balanced cantilever roof, left as it comes from the shuttering except that fascias and parapets are painted.

Below: Offices, showrooms, etc., for the motor department of the United Africa Company, Accra (architects, Kenneth Scott Associates). The main building has a show-room on the ground floor with mezzanine offices, and two office floors above. At right-angles is the storage building with new vehicles and spare-parts sales department on the ground floor and spare-parts storage above. There is a staff canteen on the roof.

Top: Museum at Accra (architects, Drake and Lasdun), designed as the first stage of a national museum and opened in March, 1957, as part of the celebrations of Ghana's independence. The interior is lit by slit windows in the saw-tooth walls (shaded by the overhanging roof) and clerestory windows beneath the dome, also lighting a gallery. Construction is reinforced concrete and rendered brick, with aluminium dome pre-fabricated in Britain.

Above: Boys' School at Apowa (architects, Fry, Drew and Partners), typical of the large number of schools and training colleges designed by these architects around 1950 for the then Gold Coast. The photograph shows the hall, chapel and administration building. Construction is reinforced concrete.

Right: Regional Library at Koforidua, for the Ghana Library Board (architects, Kenneth Scott Associates). It contains a general and children's sections, besides staffrooms, cloakrooms, stores, etc. The total area is 1,350 sq. ft. The structure is steel-framed with timber roof finished with felt on plywood decking. Partitions are concrete blocks plastered. Windows are adjustable glass louvres with a continuous strip of fixed glazing at clerestory level.

Housing at Tesano, near Accra (architects, Kenneth Scott Associates). The group of three steel-framed houses was built for a speculator and leased to the Mobiloil Company. Each has car-port, store, laundry and drying-yard on the ground floor, and on the first floor (area 2,000 sq. ft.), stoep, living-room, kitchen, two air-conditioned bedrooms and two bathrooms. Servants' quarters are separate. Floors, roofs and partitions are timber; ceilings and partition infill are plaster. Roofs are bituminous felt on wood-wool decking. Windows are steel with Venetian blinds behind the fixed panels.

Ghana

key
1, kitchen
2, yard
3, bedroom
4, living room
5, boy's room

plan of type A house.

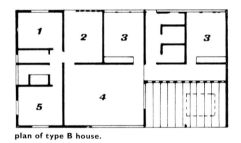

plan of type B house.

5 O   35

On this page is shown staff housing at Kumasi College of Technology (architects, James Cubitt and Partners). Other buildings of the College are shown on the next two pages.
At top: a two-bedroom type house, with car-port on the left of the frontage. Centre: the verandah of a smaller two-bedroom type, with open 'impluvium' in the roof. Right: exterior of the same house showing the heavily louvred windows needed in the humid and oppressive climate a few degrees north of the Equator.

On this and the facing page: buildings in the main teaching area of the College of Technology at Kumasi, capital of the Ashanti (architects, James Cubitt and Partners). Above: the engineering workshops, with timber roof suspended from reinforced concrete Y-beams 30 ft. apart, giving clerestory lighting above the single row of columns on which each Y-beam rests. Louvres occupy the upper part of the walls. The lower part consists of continuous pressed steel doors, partly glazed. A covered way gives shade right round the building. Below: the main teaching area from the north-east; from left to right: science block; pharmacy block; lecture-room block.

Ghana

Above: the pharmacy block in the centre of
the main teaching area of Kumasi College
of Technology; looking eastwards along the
causeway leading from the library (see plan).
It is in the main single-storey, but over the
central corridor is a narrow mezzanine
containing research laboratories and
administrative offices. A transverse wall
separates the chemistry and metallurgy
departments from the rest of the building.
The main reinforced concrete structure
consists of columns 25 ft. apart carrying deep
transverse beams and forming a colonnade
along either side of the building. The walls
are structurally independent. Lavatory blocks
on either side of the entrance, at the end
shown in the photograph, are of load-
bearing block walls roofed by a continuation
of the mezzanine slab. Below: the lecture-
room block from the south.

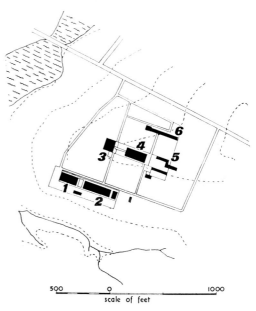

500   0   1000
scale of feet

key: 1, workshop block. 2, workshop laboratories. 3, library.
4, pharmacy. 5, science blocks. 6, lecture-room block.

Above: the north side of the science block of a secondary school at Sekondi (architects, James Cubitt and Partners). The school shares a site (see plan alongside) with a teachers' training college, but each group of buildings is self-sufficient though with certain services in common. The long, narrow site runs north and south, with a slope in a southerly direction which allows the buildings to make the most of the breeze. The structure is a reinforced concrete frame. Below: the south side of the science block.

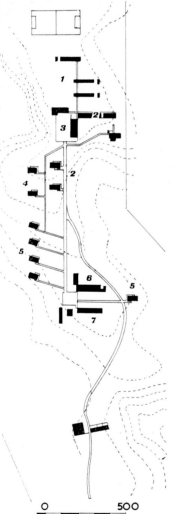

Showrooms and offices at Accra for the Industrial Development Corporation (architects, James Cubitt and Partners). The view above is of the south façade which has louvred walls to give shade.

site plan
key

Teachers' Training College

1, dormitories.
2, staff housing.
3, assembly hall.
4, classrooms.

Secondary Day School

5, staff housing.
6, science block.
7, classrooms.

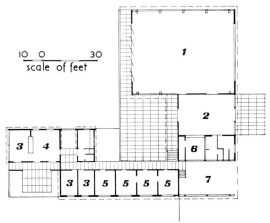

Assembly hall, Accra (architects, James
Cubitt and Partners). This hall was built as a
memorial to Gold Coast personnel killed in the
war. It contains a hall, a foyer, a bar, some
offices and a small flat for the secretary. The
building is constructed chiefly of local timber,
although for economy reasons the roof-trusses
are made of laminated timber which was
imported from Holland. The view above is of
the south (entrance) front of the assembly hall.

key: 1, hall. 2, foyer. 3, bedrooms. 4, caretaker's living room.
5, offices. 6, bar. 7, car-port.

The United States Embassy, Accra (architect, Harry Weese of Chicago). Above: the main entrance elevation. Left: the rear elevation, showing the outside service staircase. Below: inside the courtyard, showing the double-staircase leading to the first floor, at which level all the accommodation is planned, the ground floor being entirely open to allow free circulation of air. The building has a reinforced concrete frame but is otherwise designed to make the greatest possible use of the inexpensive local mahogany.

Nigeria

The British High Commissioner's official residence, Lagos (architect, Lionel Brett, commissioned by the Ministry of Works). Above: the main entrance, with part of the upper floor cantilevered out to form a porch. The coat of arms is by Edward Bawden. Behind the screen walls are garden courtyards, with the main accommodation beyond. This faces on to the lagoon (below), and on this side – the opposite side to the entrance – the residence opens out, with wide windows and the living accommodation spread along the water-front in two storeys.

Primary school, Lagos (architects, Fry, Drew, Drake and Lasdun): one of a series using multiples of four and eight classrooms in units adaptable to various sites (see plan below). Construction is reinforced concrete, with concrete block walls including pre-cast louvre blocks, and timber-framed windows.

key:
1, administration building.
2, assembly hall and meal room.
3, existing school (to be demolished).
4, classroom blocks.
5, lavatory block.

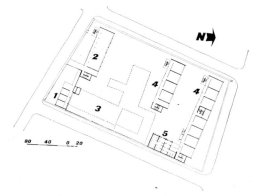

80   40   0   20

A detached bedroom block, Ikoyi hotel, Lagos (architects, Halliday and Webster – Design Group Nigeria): in the grounds of the existing hotel, providing twenty-four single and twelve double bedrooms each with its own bathroom and private balcony, reached from a central corridor. All rooms are air-conditioned. Construction is reinforced concrete with projecting panels (forming the wall of the bathrooms, which have clerestory lighting) faced with ceramic mosaic tiles.

Treasury Buildings, Ibadan (architect, J. E. K. Harrison, in association with the Ministry of Works and Transport, Nigeria Western Region): the principal government office building for the Region, with offices for the Prime Minister and his staff, a cabinet room and offices for the Ministry of Finance. Above: from the south-east, showing the large balcony outside the Prime Minister's room.

Office building on Lagos waterfront for the Co-operative Bank of Western Nigeria (architects, Fry, Drew, Drake and Lasdun). A reinforced concrete framed building, with blank travertine-faced side wall, and ground floor open for car-parking. Windows have adjustable aluminium louvres.

School at Lagos (architects, Godwin and Hopwood), a Methodist school for 1,080 boys and girls, comprising two classroom wings with a covered assembly space between. Above: the longer block, facing south, at the far end of which is a maisonette for one of the Methodist catechists. Construction is reinforced concrete with brick infill and timber and aluminium roofs.

Nigeria

key: 1, bank and tower. 2, car parking. 3, assembly hall.
, service yard. 5, roof restaurant and showroom. 6, shop.

ffice building, Ibadan (architects, Fry,
rew, Drake and Lasdun), for the
o-operative Bank of Western Nigeria. The
n-storey tower shown here has the bank on
e ground and first floors. Also on the site
ce plan) are an assembly hall seating 850
r co-operative and other functions, a shop
ing with offices over and a showroom with
staurant on roof. Construction is
inforced concrete.

Offices and showrooms in Lagos (architects, Godwin and Hopwood) built for Allen and Hanburys (Nigeria) Ltd. on the east side of Tinubu Square (left). Most of the ground floor is for car-parking. Showrooms, reception and director's office are on the first floor and above are four floors of offices. Below: one of the main elevations, protected from the low morning and evening sun by adjustable aluminium louvres, with pivoted windows behind. Construction is reinforced concrete. The concrete slab roof has an aluminium roof over it, with air-space between.

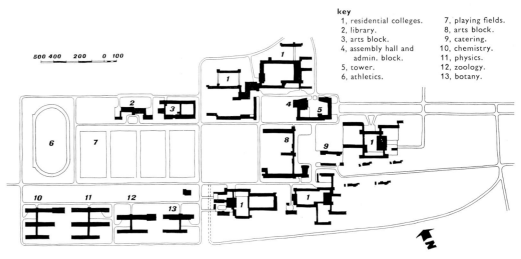

500 400 200 0 100

University College, Ibadan (architects, Fry, Drew and Partners): a complete university (see plan), on a site of five square miles. Above: one of the women's residential colleges (all of which are planned round courtyards). Left: the library, with natural cross-ventilation. It is fly-proofed behind perforated concrete screening. Left, below: housing for the senior staff.

key
1, main entrance.
2, car parks.
3, private secretaries' lodges.
4, reception.
5, wives' quarters.
6, garages.
7, kitchens.
8, servants' quarters.
9, covered way.
10, caretaker.
11, domestic block.
12, future extension.

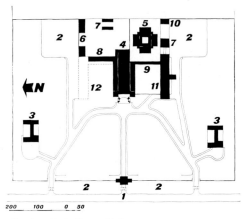

200   100   0   50

site plan: State House, Kaduna

State House, Kaduna, Northern Region (Ministry of Works, Northern Region: chief architect, J. E. Evans; architect, J. R. Greer-Perry). A symmetrical group of buildings (see site-plan) with a high reception hall in the centre flanked by a cabinet room on one side (not yet built) and the Prime Minister's offices on the other. All are linked by covered ways. Ancillary buildings enclose garden courts. Construction is reinforced concrete and concrete blocks with a steel roof to the hall.

key
1, studio.
2, cubicle.
3, 4, records.
5, testing.
6, workshop.
7, existing studio.

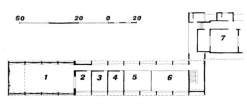

60   20   0   20

plan: broadcasting buildings, Enugu

Below: extensions to Broadcasting House, Enugu (architects, Godwin and Hopwood). A two-storey studio with technical rooms alongside (see plan), above which are offices. The main windows face south. The studio is separated from the remainder by an expansion joint. Construction is load-bearing piers of hollow blocks, filled with concrete, and reinforced concrete floor and roof beams. Roof covering is aluminium and the walls are insulated with aluminium foil. The interior is air-conditioned from a plant in a semi-basement beneath the studio.

Dock offices at Port Harcourt (architects, the Architects' Co-Partnership) for the Nigerian Ports Authority. The first floor windows are shaded on the corridor side by adjustable vertical louvres allowing full ventilation and on the office side by horizontal aluminium louvres hung from the roof beam.

House at Lagos (architects, the Architects' Co-Partnership) for the general manager of an oil company. It is planned to provide natural ventilation to the living-rooms; the bedroom wing is air-conditioned. Concrete block walls support timber roof beams and aluminium sheeting.

Below: architect's own office and residence, Lagos (architects, Godwin and Hopwood), seen from the north. On a restricted site on Lagos Island, it has four floors each divided in two and linked by a spiral stair. The two lower floors contain car-port, entrance and offices and the two upper floors a maisonette with roof-garden above. Servants' quarters are in a separate building behind. Windows are kept to a minimum on the east-west walls except on the bedroom floor which is air-conditioned. Construction is concrete and hollow blocks.

House at Ikoyi, Lagos (architects, Fry, Drew and Partners): one of three built for British Overseas Airways personnel. On the ground floor is a garage and a guest suite. Above is a two-bedroom flat with a terrace (shown in the photograph) opening from the living room. There is also a 20 feet square central open court. Construction is reinforced concrete with block walls and hardwood windows.

Nigeria

Houses at Kano (architects, James Cubitt and Partners) for Barclay's Bank. A group of semi-detached houses to which two more pairs will later be added. The near-desert climate of Kano demands protection against heat and glare, given here by a perforated screen of concrete blocks three feet in front of the south wall and a wide roof overhang on the north wall. Construction is of concrete beams and blocks with timber and asbestos roof.

Architects' own house and office at Apapa, Lagos (architects, Becker and Voigt): single-storey, with garage and boys' quarters separate. The house itself, and the office and guest wing, both facing a screened courtyard (right), are separated by a car-port (see plan below). Below: view from the south-west. Walls are load-bearing blocks; the roof is reinforced concrete and timber.

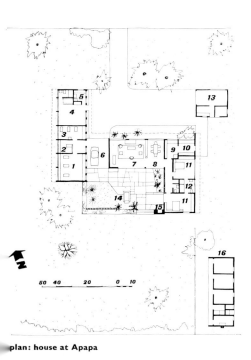

plan: house at Apapa

key

1, architects' office.	9, pantry.
2, secretary.	10, kitchen.
3, draughtsmen.	11, bedrooms.
4, guest room.	12, bath.
5, guests' kitchen.	13, garage.
6, car park.	14, shower basin.
7, living room.	15, barbecue.
8, dining room.	16, servants' quarters.

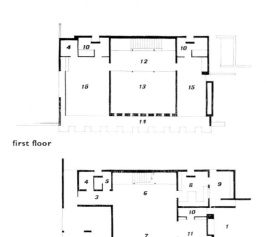

first floor

key: 1, terraces. 2, garage. 3, lobby. 4, stores. 5, lavatories. 6, dining area. 7, living area. 8, kitchen. 9, laundry yard. 10, bathrooms. 11, study. 12, bridge. 13, upper part of living room. 14, balcony. 15, bedrooms.

```
30   20   10    0    10
```

ground floor plan of house at Kano

House at Kano (architects, the Architects' Co-Partnership), designed for the hot dry climate of this region. The ground floor walls are of rubble stone 18 in. thick and have small openings, providing protection from high daytime temperatures. Heat from such walls, however, radiates after sundown into the interior of the house, so a light structure has been used on the first floor, composed of steel rods and aluminium sheeting, the high conductivity of which quickly disperses at sundown the heat absorbed during the day.

EAST AFRICA AS A REGION consists of four territories, distinct from one another in historical and political development, climatic and geographic characteristics and economic levels. These factors affect their architectural character no less than do the differences in procedure for the registration of architects.

Zanzibar, the smallest and most isolated of the units in the region, is still in the grip of a strong Arabic influence. The island is ruled by a hereditary Sultan, part of a tradition which includes the architecture, with arcaded courtyards and white walls, embellished with complex tracery, purple-shadowed in the strong sun. The narrow streets, overhung with intricately carved balconies, and lined with blank walls punctuated by carved doors, massive and black with age, apparently create too strong an atmosphere for modern architecture – banks, petrol stations and even the airport are built with moorish arches and traceried balconies. One should add that lack of space in the town of Zanzibar makes new buildings of any style comparatively rare.

Tanganyika, the largest in area and population of the East African territories, is in many ways the most interesting. Politically Tanganyika, under the leadership of Julius Nyerere, is closer to responsible self-government than either Kenya or Uganda, and with less bitterness and controversy between the various racial groups. The legacy of German colonial architecture, with improbably slender cast-iron columns supporting wide first-floor verandahs and white-painted louvred shutters with black trim, is a valuable one to the coastal towns of Tanganyika.

Since the war, new buildings in Dar es Salaam, as in Mombasa farther to the north, have mostly been covered with concrete louvres or egg-crate brise-soleil, in an attempt to keep out direct rays of the sun. The general economic level of the country does not allow many entirely air-conditioned buildings, which could be designed as such, or more sophisticated adjustable types of sun-screening which would provide better conditions and more interesting and intricate elevational patterns. The result is a certain heaviness and crudity. An allied factor is that standards of workmanship are such that buildings must be designed down to the level of the craftsmen available. Other than simple screening of the sun's rays, there has been little exploration of climatic design. The hot and humid conditions to be found along the coast affect Mombasa, Tanga and Dar es Salaam. A characteristic of this climate is little diurnal and annual range: the mean maximum and minimum temperatures for Mombasa are 86° and 72°, with a mean humidity of 80 per cent. Towns such as Kisumu, Entebbe and Kampala, on the shores of Lake Victoria, also have a hot and humid climate, but not so extreme.

Tanganyika had early contact with modern architecture as practised in Europe. The town of Moshi, on the slopes of Kilimanjaro, the highest mountain in Africa, derives its considerable prosperity from the enterprising Chagga tribe, who some years ago were persuaded to grow coffee as a cash crop, and set up a co-operative union to market the produce. They built a headquarters building for the union and a number of clinics, schools, district offices and houses, which were designed by Dr Ernst May, the famous German town planner, and his partners. Dr May himself has now returned to Germany.

Another link with the modern architectural movement in Europe of the 'twenties and 'thirties is the work of A. D. Connell (formerly of Connell, Ward and Lucas). He designed a number of interesting private houses and low-cost housing schemes in and around the port of Tanga between 1947 and 1954, when he moved to Nairobi.

In Uganda any architecture of note is concentrated for the most part in Kampala, which spreads over a number of hilltops, the crests being capped with the hospital, cathedral, mosque and Kabaka's palace. The hills, with the hot and humid climate and luxuriant vegetation, give Kampala a character of its own. This is enhanced by being the seat of an hereditary ruler, the Kabaka of Buganda, and the commercial capital (Entebbe on the lake-shore is the administrative capital) of a prosperous African state.

Uganda has self-government within reach as soon as the various factions in the country can come to agreement on the details. As in East Africa generally, the greatest volume of building is commissioned by the Asian community, but to a large extent to other than qualified or registered architects. This is made even easier in Uganda than elsewhere, as the Protectorate has no ordinance controlling the use of the title 'architect'. In Kenya and Tanganyika this is restricted to those whose qualifications satisfy the Board of Registration, although this does not prevent firms of 'building engineers', 'building consultants', 'designers' and others carrying on a flourishing trade, with reduced fees and professional standards. This has had a marked effect on the visual environment of East African towns, as more than half the non-government work is designed by other than qualified architects. The effect is, for the most part, crude and garish, with bizarre colouring and outmoded clichés, and the planning is often wasteful and inconvenient.

Kenya is the most complex of the East African territories: politically confused, geographically varied and economically viable. The vast majority of East African architects practise in Kenya, and most of those in Nairobi. There are firms in Mombasa, Nakuru, Kisumu and Kitale, but most of the work, both in the capital and the country as a whole, is carried out by Nairobi architects.

In Nairobi's growing suburbs, the older pattern of orange mangalore tiles, 9-in. coursed dull grey stone and metal windows, with the inevitable small replica for servants at the end of the garden, is not now so frequent. The stridently modernistic work of the 'designers' has made the public more receptive to good modern design as being comparatively mild. Most private houses built in Nairobi today could loosely be described as contemporary, although too many reflect a superficial culling of the architectural magazines, rather than a genuine style appropriate to the country.

Nairobi is one of the few cities that has adhered, in the main, to its town plan, which was prepared in 1947 by Professor Thornton White. The plan had to recognize the existing sprawl of the city and also did little to integrate the vast areas of African housing with other residential areas. The acres of low-cost and low-standard African housing which form a large part of any East African town, lie unrelated to the life of the town itself, but always present. The plan has, however, given the new commercial and administrative centre some coherence and order without regimentation, although the regimentation of the international style has engulfed Nairobi, as it has most other cities. In East Africa, stainless steel and porcelain curtain-walling becomes standard metal windows with painted (or coloured mosaic) spandrels in a grid of concrete mullions. The rectangular block is framed and lifted off the ground as in Canberra, Chicago or Caracas. The East African climate, however, requires less window-area and deep reveals or sun-screening, rather than the continuous window this style demands; for even in towns with a relatively temperate climate, such as Nairobi, Moshi and Nakuru, the brightness of the sky and sun is excessive for the greater part of the year. These towns, at altitudes of 4,000 feet to 6,000 feet, have a mild climate, with day temperatures rarely above 80° or below 65° and cool nights, the lowest recorded night temperature for Nairobi being 44°.

Local materials are limited: asbestos, concrete tiles and shingles are available locally, as is stone, some brick and hollow blocks, both clay and concrete. Portland cement and standard metal doors and windows are produced by East African factories. Practically all other materials and equipment, apart from timber (but including hardboard, softboard, plywood, etc.), have to be imported, mainly from Europe. This keeps building costs up and causes endless delays and frustration when local agents are out of stock of special fittings and materials.

A growing field of work, which could break away from both the traditional and international styles, is that commissioned by African dominated organizations. Many African district councils are building office blocks and council halls; parish committees are starting new churches, the Chagga Coffee Co-operative has already been mentioned and, also in Tanganyika, the Cotton Co-operative has commissioned new offices. Another new project is Tom Mboya's Kenya Federation of Labour headquarters in Nairobi. This new class of client neither recognizes nor wants European traditions, particularly of the village green type, but he does want something good, up-to-date and vigorous which will reflect his hopes for a new Africa.

The majority of architects in East Africa are Europeans, with a number of

Asian firms. All these firms are based in the country, and their principals and assistants regard themselves as East Africans, having permanently settled in East Africa. Most of the older generation were born and trained in Britain, but there is a growing number of young European and Asian (and there is now one African) architects who were born in East Africa, have trained abroad and returned to practice, sometimes in their father's firm. In this rapidly developing area, this pattern is already changing in that there is now a Faculty of Architecture in the Royal Technical College of East Africa (soon to be part of a University of East Africa) which has some twenty-five students in the first four years.

The Faculty was founded in 1956 and runs a course aimed at producing a qualified architect in seven years. The first three years up to RIBA Intermediate are similar to courses in British schools. The second stage consists of one-and-a-half years of full-time studio work, one year in an architect's office, followed by six months revision in the College before taking the RIBA finals. Whether a student can develop the breadth of vision and recognition of the highest standards in architecture, when he has been educated entirely in a small country, isolated from the traditions of the past and the best of the present, remains to be seen. In any case, the demands of a fast developing region are such that architects from Europe will still be needed for many years to come.

RICHARD HUGHES

Kenya

An architect's own house at Nairobi (architect, H. Richard Hughes), designed to use a very steep site in a way that would separate the house into units (see plan and section). The living rooms are at entrance level but on the north side, where there is a view to the forest beyond, they are one floor up. The study, hall and bathroom form a link with the bedroom wing, which is a few feet higher. This has been planned for future expansion. The stone spine screens the backyard and servants' quarters from the entrance. Walls are concrete blocks; roofs are timber. Above: from the east, showing space beneath living-room which has now been walled in to form a drawing-office. Right: the dining-room, with view over the forest.

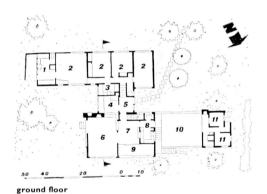

ground floor

section

key
1, dressing room.
2, bedrooms.
3, bathroom.
4, study.
5, hall.
6, living room.
7, dining room.
8, kitchen.
9, balcony.
10, yard.
11, servants.

Asian housing, Nairobi (architect, Idris Davies):
a group of identical blocks of municipal flats
with staircase access, each with two flats on
each of four storeys.

Kenya

Aga Khan hospital, Nairobi (architect, A. D. Connell). The illustration shows the south front of the four-storey ward block (four large and four small wards at each level totalling 120 beds). Behind it, linked to the ward block by a glazed lobby, is a fan-shaped service and operating block flanked by ramps leading to the upper floors of both blocks. Service circulation runs beneath it.

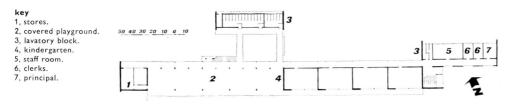

key
1, stores.
2, covered playground.
3, lavatory block.
4, kindergarten.
5, staff room.
6, clerks.
7, principal.

50 40 30 20 10 0 10

plan of girls' school, Parklands.

Arya girls' senior school at Parklands, Nairobi (architects, T. G. Gedrych and Peer Abben): a two-storey building with ground floor partly open (see plan above) of concrete construction with rubble stone ground floor walls.

Kenya

Right: cinema in Government Road, Nairobi (architects, Blaker and McCullough), photographed at night and showing the illuminated interior behind the all-glass façade. The panel behind the lettering is of ceramic mosaic. Construction is reinforced concrete with a steel truss roof.

Left: Kenya Federation of Labour headquarters. Nairobi (architect, H. Richard Hughes): from the south-west. The building, for Tom Mboya's trade unions, sited in the African part of Nairobi, has offices on the upper floor and is designed for the addition of a second office floor later. The assembly hall shown on the ground floor plan below has also not yet been built. Construction is load-bearing stone piers, U-shaped for stability, with reinforced concrete floor and roof slabs.

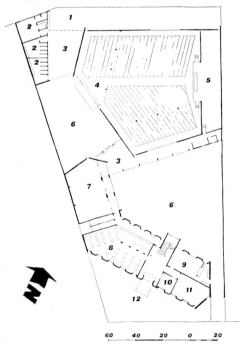

key

1, car park.
2, lavatories.
3, covered ways.
4, assembly hall.
5, platform.
6, courtyards.
7, classrooms.
8, library.
9, canteen.
10, reception.
11, office.
12, main entrance.

60 40 20 0 20

ground floor plan, headquarters
for Kenya Federation of Labour

Below: terminal buildings, Nairobi Airport (architects, Kenya Ministry of Works): the main entrance leading into the passenger concourse. Beyond the latter are the customs hall and waiting lounges and, on the far side, the aircraft standings. On the left can be seen a two-storey block of offices, etc., surrounding a garden court, beyond which are a restaurant and the control-tower.

Crown law offices, Nairobi (architect, A. D. Connell), a five-storey building with its whole north-west façade (shown in the photograph) and the corresponding façade on the opposite side covered by a concrete grille for sun-protection. The openings in the grille coincide with alternate windows behind, which are centrally pivoted. The upper floors contain offices either side of a central corridor, with a first-floor conference room the full width of the building at the far end and a two-storey library above it. The louvred ground floor wall shown in the photograph marks the end of a single-storey public office projecting at right-angles behind the main building, with domed roof-lights.

Coffee mills and warehouse, Nairobi (architect, Blackburne Norburn): a complex of buildings constructed over several years for the Kenya Planters' Co-operative Union. The newest part is that on the right: an additional mill block with dust-house in front of it. In the centre is a storage block connected to a warehouse by a bridge. An auction-hall also forms part of the scheme.

Office building, Nairobi (architects, Jackson and Hill): an eight-storey curtain-walled block, typical of those now being constructed in the central business area.

upper floor plan

ground floor plan

Police Officers' mess and flats, Kampala (architect, C. G. Andrews, chief architect, Public Works Department; assistants-in-charge, J. S. Fuller and W. A. Schwartzel). The main three-storey building accommodates ten bachelors and two families. The single-storey mess (see plan) has lounge-dining room, bar, billiard-room and services. The flats have a reinforced concrete frame with hollow pot concrete floors and roof. The mess has load-bearing walls with a hollow pot concrete roof of butterfly shape.

key. 1, entrance. 2, lounge-dining room. 3, terrace. 4, bar. 5, bar service. 6, laundry. 7, kitchen. 8, kitchen service. 9, ladies room. 10, office. 11, billiard room. 12, bachelor flat. 13, married couple's flat.

Bank and offices, Kampala, for the Uganda Credit and Savings Bank (architects, Inglis, McGuinness and Wilkinson), comprising a main banking-hall with covered side entrance and an office block at right-angles attached to one end (on left in photograph). The banking-hall has a mezzanine gallery at the rear containing the senior executives' offices. A second gallery, running the length of the hall, forms a canopy over the counter and tellers' booths and provides storage for files. The hall is top-lit by dome-lights with heat-resisting glass. The strong-rooms are in the basement.

Office block, Owen Falls hydro-electric
scheme (architect, H. L. Ford;
consulting engineers, Sir Alexander
Gibb and Partners): for the Uganda
Electricity Board. The four-storey
building adjoins the power station with
road access at two levels and contains
offices, control-room, cable-chamber,
canteens and welfare accommodation.
Construction is reinforced concrete
with deep exterior columns on north
and south elevations to shade the walls
and windows. Wall-facing is pre-cast
concrete slabs with local granite
aggregate.

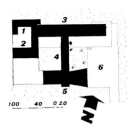

site plan, school at Mbale
key
1, kitchen.
2, workshops.
3, living accommodation.
4, administration.
5, teaching block.
6, car park.

School of Hygiene, Mbale (architect,
John Falconer of Deans and Partners)
for the Director of Public Works: a
residential school for 120 adult students
being trained as health inspectors, etc.
The photograph shows two storeys of
dormitories and study-bedrooms above
a ground-floor common-room. On the
left is the administration wing.

Uganda

Residential secondary school (Teso College, Aloet) near Soroti, a hot, barren and rocky part of Uganda (architect, John Falconer of Deans and Partners). The buildings (see plan), accommodating 240 boys, are planned round a square on a flat site. The photograph shows the library and administration from the west, with the assembly-hall beyond.

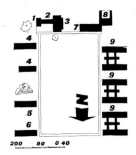

key: 1, library. 2, administration. 3, assembly hall. 4, classroom blocks. 5, practical rooms. 6, laboratories. 7, dining hall. 8, kitchen. 9, dormitory blocks.

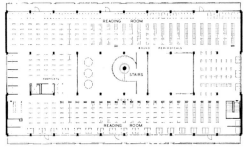

Makerere College: main floor

Library at Makerere College (the University College of East Africa) near Kampala (architects, Norman and Dawbarn). It houses 120,000 books and 300 readers and includes binding, printing and photographic departments. The plan (see main floor above) consists of two two-storey units separated by two courts, one open and one covered to form the stair and catalogue hall. The service rooms are in a lower ground floor. The library floors have verandahs along the two long sides screened by pierced ceramic grilles (see photograph of main entrance). The building has a reinforced concrete frame. The end walls are of pre-cast concrete slabs with large windows protected by metal louvres.

National Theatre and cultural centre, Kampala (architects, Peatfield and Bodgener). The theatre seats 400 and the building (see plan below) also contains offices, libraries and accommodation for various cultural societies. Construction is a reinforced concrete frame faced with terrazzo slabs and grilles incorporating East African white marble chips. Behind the grilles the window walls are in local cedar framing.

key: 1, auditorium. 2, stage. 3, green room. 4, dressing rooms. 5, office entrance hall. 6, box office. 7, entrance foyer. 8, bar foyer. 9, manager's office.

ground floor plan, National Theatre, Kampala

Right: cricket grandstand at the headquarters of the Uganda Sports Union, Kampala (architects, Peatfield and Bodgener; engineer, Colin Harris). It seats 1,200 and has a cantilevered roof clad with Kenya red cedar and covered with asbestos sheeting on teak joists. Seating is pre-cast concrete.

Right: office building (Amber House), Kampala (architects, Moross and Graff). On a steeply sloping site in the centre of Kampala, it houses the Uganda Electricity Board and the Lint and Coffee Marketing Boards. Three-, four- and five-storey wings are planned for maximum air circulation and protection from the east and west sun. A basement garage parks 100 cars. The reinforced concrete frame is clad with white and grey pre-cast terrazzo slabs.

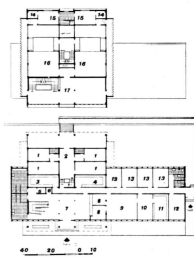

ground and first floor: magistrates' court, Kampala

Magistrates' courts, Kampala (architect, C. G. Andrews, chief architect Public Works Department; assistant-in-charge, J. E. C. Callaghan). The building adjoins the new police headquarters and contains four small courts. They are on the first and second floors (see plans) with the entrance-hall, offices and cells on the ground floor. The building has a reinforced concrete frame. Concrete grilles and louvres protect the main rooms from the sun.

key: 1, cells. 2, duty room. 3, court exhibits. 4, police exhibits. 5, meters. 6, telephone. 7, entrance hall. 8, public reception. 9, general office. 10, chief clerk. 11, library. 12, advocates. 13, offices. 14, stores. 15, magistrates. 16, courts. 17, public waiting.

Village market at Kiwafu, near Entebbe (architect, Robert Browning) for the African Housing Division, Ministry of Social Development. It serves a village estate where Africans can buy a plot of land and build their own semi-traditional houses, mostly of mud and wattle. The roofs, of locally made asbestos-cement sheeting, have tubular supports which also serve as rainwater-pipes. Walls are concrete blocks. Construction was by direct labour supervised by an African engineering assistant.

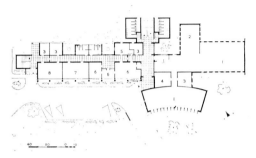

Technical institute, Dar es Salaam (architect, A. B. Almeida): the main classroom and administrative block, flanked by the single-storey reference library and reading room, with projecting entrance hall – see plan alongside. Behind is a hostel block.

key: 1, library. 2, stacking room. 3, store. 4, bookbinding. 5, bursar. 6, office. 7, staff room. 8, committee room.

European primary school, Dar es Salaam (architects, C. A. Bransgrove and Partners): from the main approach, with covered play area on left (classrooms over) and two-storey classroom wing on right. There are eight classrooms altogether, all with pierced walls of pre-cast concrete blocks to give through-ventilation, together with staff-rooms, cloakrooms and (on the second floor) two staff flats. The frame is reinforced concrete.

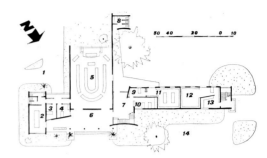

Above: local government headquarters, Singida (architects, French and Hastings; built under supervision of the Tanganyika Public Works Department): from the north. The entrance verandah, with public gallery over, leads into the council chamber – see plan. On one side are committee-rooms, etc.; on the other a two-storey wing of offices and stores. The prevailing wind is south or south-east.

key

1, members' car park.
2, committee room.
3, 4, cloaks.
5, council chamber.
6, entrance.
7, hall.
8, lavatories.

9, medical superintendent.
10, correspondence.
11, medical store.
12, equipment store.
13, foreman.
14, visitors' car park.

Left: terminal building, Dar es Salaam airport (architects, Public Works Department). It handles 5,000 passengers a month. On the ground floor are the departure, waiting and customs halls and airline offices; on the first floor a restaurant, bar, kitchen and meteorological offices; on the second floor, radio control. Walls are load-bearing concrete block and floors pre-cast reinforced concrete T-beams. The control-tower is air-conditioned.

Below: Goan Institute, Dar es Salaam (architect, A. B. Almeida): a club for the Goan community. Main rooms overlook an enclosed garden, which has a sunk open-air dance floor (see plan). Construction is reinforced concrete with concrete block walls and perforated and louvred concrete screens.

key: 1, commercial premises. 2, club office. 3, committee room, 4, table tennis room. 5, store. 6, children's play area. 7, open-air dance floor. 8, bandstand.

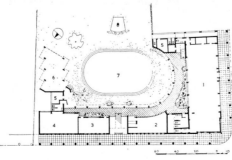

ground floor: Goan Institute

DURING THE LAST TWELVE YEARS the growth of building in the Rhodesias, which with Nyasaland form the Federation, has been remarkable. The cement-rendered shanties with corrugated iron roofs, the neo-Georgian 'official' buildings and the smattering of sham Cape Dutch, have given way to the modern buildings of ten, twenty and more storeys which now overshadow the 'tin shacks' of the pioneers. Yet the transformation of style, quality of material, general amenities and know-how has happened so quickly that people have had little time to think. Developments have been rushed ahead by force of circumstances, and a trail of problems, some serious, has been created which will have to be resolved. Too rapid development does not produce the best results, and this can be said of the majority of the towns in the Rhodesias. The slowing down of the tempo over the past three years, though it may be only a passing phase, has not been wholly a bad thing, and the country has time now to have a breather and do some re-thinking.

The Rhodesias are in the sub-tropics, on a land-locked plateau some 5,000 feet above the sea. In the dry season, the winter temperatures are low enough to need fires at night, and rise during the day into the 'seventies. This is followed by high winds and a gradual rise in temperature into the 'nineties, bringing small whirlwinds known as 'dust devils' to tear off roofs, and the hot 'suicide' month of October when tempers are at straining point. Eventually the weather breaks, accompanied by thunderstorms and intermittent torrential rain. In spite of this, it is a fine healthy climate.

Climate conditions the physical elements of building. There is need for protection from the hot west afternoon sun, the heavy rains, and the cool persistent winds of spring. Living rooms are orientated to face the north sun in the winter months, and bedrooms to catch the cool night winds. Yet perhaps the most important need is the suppression of glare from both the sky and from sunlight reflected from the ground. To combat the effects of glare on domestic and working conditions usually involves capital outlay, but deserves special consideration when measured in terms of comfort and efficiency. It is fortunate that vegetation grows so quickly to form background screens. It is common for trees to reach a height of twenty feet in four years from seed.

Now that Africans are living in towns in large numbers, a complex of social, economic and human problems has come with the appearance of the urban African. Cut off from his traditional way of village life, he has to make for himself a fundamentally new kind of existence in unfamiliar surroundings.

The African himself should be best suited to evolve a style of building to meet both the temperament and the conditions of his urban counterpart; but there is here a gulf in architectural feeling that has yet to be bridged successfully, owing to the complete lack of African architects. The majority of the architects in the Federation were born and trained in the British Isles and South Africa, and it is not surprising to find that the influence of their early environment has found expression in their buildings, and that a typical Rhodesian architecture has not yet developed. Yet it is only the past twelve years that has seen this prodigious initial development in building take place, and it is possible that the growth of a recognizable Rhodesian expression will soon be discernible.

Nature is hard in Central Africa. Hardwood trees grow with foliage at the upper level like knurled umbrellas out of reach of the bush fires that kill the growth below. Wood-eating termites live under the ground in their millions, and can endanger foundations when building their nests. The ground in summer is as hard as concrete and splits in the dry heat. Bathing in the rivers is dangerous for fear of contracting bilharzia which eats away one's intestines. One expects rugged conditions in Africa, and one would expect the European buildings to be different to those in temperate climates. Yet, go to the suburbs of any town in the Rhodesias and the general run of houses is fundamentally like those one will find in England and South Africa. Perhaps this shows the European's desire to turn his back on a natural environment that is foreign to his inherent background. The wild flowers in the bush have very vivid colours to counteract the strong sunlight that drains the colour from vegetation. As a parallel, it is noticeable how Africans like to wear bright clothes, and colours are used on buildings that would be considered harsh in temperate climates.

The car is an essential and not a luxury of life, as public transport in the towns is either non-existent or very limited. Shopping is a necessity disliked by most people, as it is hot, dusty and tiring. Car-parking is an elusive business, and except where use can be made of multi-stores of the cheaper kind, shops may be scattered over a wide area. The local authorities encourage the building of canopies over pavements – it is also good business for the shops – yet no town has developed shopping precincts for pedestrians, where cars are excluded, and shopping can be done within a limited area and with the minimum of fatigue.

The distinction in the composition of the building trade in the two Rhodesias is that the North employs European foremen with Africans as 'boss-boys', tradesmen and labourers (except in the specialist trades), whereas Africans are not allowed to work as tradesmen in towns in Southern Rhodesia. This has forced building techniques in the North to take account of the low degree of skill of the African, and imposes limitations in design and execution. The African is progressing rapidly, however, and with the general improvement in local building materials, more advanced designs are now possible.

The basic building materials are found locally. Some excellent facing bricks are now made in Southern Rhodesia, but the common brick of the Rhodesias is still of poor quality, and there are no standards for strength, porosity or size; in fact, the lack of standards for materials generally makes building a more complex and hazardous operation, and adds to the eventual cost of maintenance. River and 'dambo' sand, lime and sandstone, iron ore, asbestos and coal are all found locally. Conifers are difficult to grow because of destruction by termites (though they are now being grown in Southern Rhodesia) and are expensive to import. Local hardwoods are not used to any great extent, due to lack of facilities for seasoning and their extreme hardness in most cases. South Africa provides many of the finished building products, but these are now being manufactured to an ever-increasing extent in the Rhodesias. The high cost of transport of imported materials, due to the long distances incurred, can increase the cost of building disproportionately. It is a challenge to the architect to adapt himself to the limitations of materials, labour, constructional equipment and finance.

It is invigorating to live in a young country and to feel that, in spite of mistakes, one has a share in its growth. The Rhodesias have a sufficiently long period of development and experience behind them to weigh up their mistakes and good points, and the next decade may well be vital to the future pattern of development. High buildings are a commonplace, and only the beginnings of what is to come. There are misgivings about the capability of the new grid towns to be able to absorb the traffic as the population and number of vehicles increase. It is not unusual for Europeans to have two cars, and Africans are beginning to become car-owners. There is a feeling that there is no live 'heart' in the towns, and a lack of character in the suburbs which are apt to sprawl, and open spaces to disappear. The majority of houses are single-storey with large gardens, a legacy from the days when land was easily obtainable and the saying was, 'Oh, but there is the whole of Africa to build in.' Economic forces are changing this attitude. The old parts of the towns are being rebuilt and concrete is replacing pisé and corrugated iron. The pattern is taking shape and has come to stay.

R. K. RUTHERFORD

147

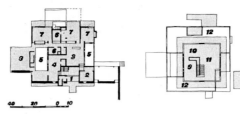

key

1, entrance.	7, bedrooms.
2, study.	8, garage.
3, family room.	9, dining.
4, kitchen.	10, music.
5, courts.	11, living.
6, bathrooms.	12, terraces.

plans of house at Ndola

House at Ndola (architect, Julian Elliott; supervising architects, Gluckman, de Beer and Peters). The site slopes to the east and towards the view. The ground floor (see plans) comprises a self-contained family unit for everyday use, with direct access to the garden and a series of enclosed courts. Over it is a suite of larger rooms for more formal use, planned round a service core, with sliding doors leading on to terraces.

key
1, car port.	7, balcony.
2, court.	8, sitting area.
3, future room.	9, dining area.
4, servant.	10, kitchen.
5, laundry.	11, children's room.
6, lavatory.	12, bathroom.
	13, bedroom.

Above: the architect's own house at Ndola (architect, H. Cameron-Smith of W. D'Arcy Cathcart & Son), on a wooded site orientated to take advantage of distant easterly views. The core of the 28-ft. square plan (above) is a large brick chimney containing flues from barbecue and servants' quarters below and living room fireplace. Screen wall between kitchen and dining space is also brick. Construction otherwise is steel (staircase and roof-ridge) and timber.

Below: garage at Broken Hill (architect, Julian Elliott; assistant in charge, Neil Grobbelaar; engineers, Ove Arup and Partners). Showrooms, spare-part store and workshops are planned round a central administrative core (see plan on right) with service core beneath. The tubular steel roof is a spine-girder with balanced cantilevers supported on shaped concrete columns and forming a parasol independent of internal partitions, allowing flexibility of sub-division. The roof is covered with corrugated iron, with translucent sheets designed to equalize the intensity of light in the showroom with that outside and so avoid reflections in the glass wall. The ceiling is expanded metal, through which the light passes, and the underside of the roof is partly seen.

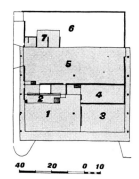

40   20   0 10

Garage: Broken Hill

key
1, showroom.	4, store.
2, office.	5, workshop.
3, outdoor display.	6, yard.
	7, service bay.

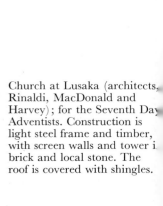

Church at Lusaka (architects, Rinaldi, MacDonald and Harvey); for the Seventh Day Adventists. Construction is light steel frame and timber, with screen walls and tower i brick and local stone. The roof is covered with shingles.

Municipal library at Lusaka (architects, Rinaldi, MacDonald and Harvey). The building was still unfinished when photographed. Left: detail of the link, with a patterned concrete grille, between the main library ar the hall. Below: the entranc side showing hall on left anc the main first floor reading-room on right. Construction is a reinforced concrete fran with pre-cast slab walling above and narrow brick walling below, pierced as shown on left.

Ridgeway Hotel, Lusaka (architect, Geoffrey A. Jellicoe). The site is a tree-clad spur of a hill above the lower town. Bedrooms occupy the two upper floors, planned in two parallel wings, below which is the reception area, the main lounge and the offices, etc. The other public rooms are single-storey. The wing projecting into the foreground of the photograph contains the ballroom, and, beyond it, are the bedroom wings and central water tower. On the other side there is a restaurant with open-air verandah overlooking a pool. Construction is reinforced concrete with brick infill panels, rendered externally and colour-washed pink. Roofs are timber covered with asbestos sheeting. Interior decoration and furnishing are by Denis Lennon.

typical upper floor plan

key
1, pantry.
2, manager's bedroom.
3, manager's sitting room.
4, sitting room.
5, double bedroom.
6, single bedroom.
7, linen.
8, housekeeper.

the future extension is shaded

Office building (Caravelle House), Ndola, with bookshop and restaurant on
the ground floor (architects, Gluckman, de Beer and Peters; supervising
architect, Julian Elliott). The four floors of offices face north-west and are
protected from the sun by a continuous projecting fascia of heat-absorbing
glass, sub-divided by aluminium frames and cantilevered from the face of the
wall on aluminium brackets. Horizontal louvres allow heated air to escape
up the face of the building, and also allow windows to be open when it is
raining. Walling between windows is in grey terrazzo brick.

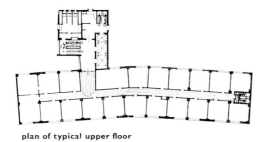

plan of typical upper floor

Office building (Compensation House), Salisbury, for the Workmen's Insurance Fund (architects, Driver-Jowitt and Lincoln): a semi-government project, forming the first part of an official centre straddling the main street of Salisbury. The curved main block (see plan above) is orientated to avoid direct sunlight. The covered entrance leads to an industrial court on the ground floor, with offices above which include those of the Federal Prime Minister; also the Cabinet room. Window façades have yellow-bronze metal panels and blue mosaic, and steel windows with dark-tinted glass. Other façades are mosaic and terrazzo.

Office building (Trustee House), Salisbury, partly for an investment and property company, partly for letting (architects, John Gauldie and Partners). The ground floor has shops and parking space. The tower block faces north with a view over a public park. Cladding is brick. Boxed screens protect windows from the sun. All office accommodation is air-conditioned.

Building society offices, Salisbury (architects, Feit and Meyers, in association with Toung, Morgenstern and Morgenstern of Johannesburg). The ground floor has a banking-hall and shops. The upper floors (except for the tenth, where the society has its executive office) are planned for separate letting. The main tower block of eleven floors faces north and south. The plan is based on a four-foot module. The main façades have brushed terrazzo fins, steel windows and pressed steel spandrel panels, with a sculptured reconstructed stone facing to the tower. The shop fronts and banking-hall are finished in granite and bronze.

Office building (Robinson House) in the centre of Salisbury
(architects, Feit and Meyers, in association with Toung,
Morgenstern and Morgenstern of Johannesburg). The
ground floor has shops on the two street-frontages and the
basement a car-park. The main tower of fourteen office
floors has north-south aspect; the lower wing at right angles
has four office floors. Planning is on a four-foot module.
Construction is reinforced concrete with flat slab floors.
The north and west façades have terrazzo fins and spandrel
panels and all windows are protected from the sun by
steel horizontal louvres.

Car showroom and garage, Bulawayo (architects, Berlowitz and Furmanovsky; engineers, Ove Arup and Partners). The building occupies a whole block of Jameson Street, and contains showroom, spares department, used-car showroom, battery shop, stores, workshop, service-line and filling station and offices. It is one of the largest of its kind in Africa. To meet the need for minimum changes in floor level, ramps take up a 6-ft. fall in the site and mezzanine floors are introduced at the lower end. The photograph shows, from left to right, ramp entrance to upper-level car-store, and service-line entrance and exit. Construction is reinforced concrete with brick panel-walls on the upper floor and stressed-skin roof in steel.

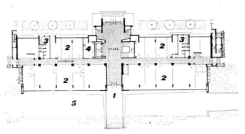

ground floor plan: Rhodesia Railways offices
key: 1, bridge. 2, offices. 3, lavatories. 4, messengers. 5, ramp to basement.

Above and facing page: headquarter offices for Rhodesia Railways, Bulawayo (railway architect, H. Billiard; assistant architect, C. E. Plews): in Metcalfe Square, overlooking the Park. It is the first stage of a much larger scheme. A basement car-park is reached by a ramp, which the main entrance bridges over – see illustration and plan. Above are seven floors of offices and a top floor with motor-rooms, etc., on which a cafeteria will be added later. Construction is a reinforced concrete frame with brick infilling.

Offices for Rhodesia
Railways, Bulawayo
(see also foot of
facing page): detail
of the stairs on the end
walls, which face east
and west.

Right: Ambassador Hotel, Salisbury (architect, Albert Ruddiman). A 20-storey extension of the old hotel, which can be seen in the foreground, and will later be demolished and replaced. The five lower floors only of the present extension are used for hotel purposes, the remainder being Government offices. Construction is reinforced concrete.

Below: flats at Salisbury (architects, Rinaldi, Macdonald and Harvey): a group of six identical blocks, laid out in parallel formation, on the fringe of the central business area. The ground floor of each block is occupied by garages.

Control and office building of the Kariba Hydro-Electric scheme, which is a Federal project situated on the Zambesi River (architect, H. L. Ford; engineers, Alexander Gibb, Coyne and Sogei). The building, shown here from the north-east, contains the main control room and the offices of the Federal Power Board, which include a demonstration room for film shows, etc., and also an observation room cantilevered over the Kariba gorge. The reinforced concrete frame has walling of precast slabs and stone obtained locally.

Rhodes National Gallery, Salisbury (architects, Montgomerie and Oldfield). The building was the result of a competition. A large double-storey multi-purpose gallery is surrounded by storage rooms at ground level and a library and more gallery-space at first floor level – see plan on the right. A ramp links the two levels, on both of which there is exhibition space in the open air. The building is constructed of reinforced concrete, and it has an exposed tubular steel roof enclosing top lights.

ground floor plan, Rhodes National Gallery

key: 1, entrance. 2, main gallery. 3, storage. 4, open court. 5, open-air display. 6, office. 7, lavatory. 8, workshops. 9, air-conditioning room. 10, African changing room. 11, strong room. 12, pool.

Left: factory at Bulawayo, producing paper bags, containers, waxed paper, etc. (architects, Rinaldi, Macdonald and Harvey): designed for maximum flexibility of plant and layout. Shown here is the south elevation of the main production hall, constructed with portal frames in concrete, filled with brick panel walls and glazing.

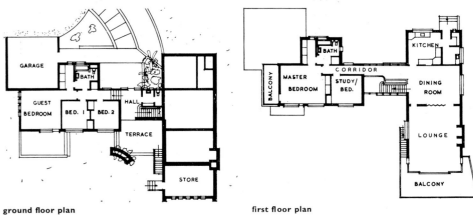

ground floor plan   first floor plan

Southern Rhodesia

House at Salisbury (architects, A. Lloyd Spencer and Partners), built on the top of a small but steep hill, with a cantilevered balcony designed to make the most of beautiful views over the Unwinisidale Valley. The main living-room has sliding windows, seen in the top illustration, opening on to the balcony. The upper floor of the bedroom wing (see plans above) opens off a gallery over the living-room; the lower floor is reached up a small flight of steps from the entrance-hall.

The Caribbean

UNTIL RECENTLY WHEN ONE SPOKE of the British West Indies one meant the British colonies of the Caribbean and also the mainland dependencies of British Guiana, in South America, and British Honduras, in Central America. In 1958 a Federation, under the style, The British West Indies, came into being. It comprises the British island colonies, but not the two mainland territories, although they are associated with the Federation in a number of regional activities. The federated territories, bordering the Caribbean Sea, stretch in an arc of over 1,000 miles from Jamaica, south of Cuba, to Trinidad, north-east of Venezuela. The Bahamas and Bermuda are sometimes described as part of the West Indies; they are not part of the Federation and strictly speaking are North Atlantic territories, not Caribbean.

The population of the West Indies exceeds three million. Over one-half live in Jamaica, the largest island; but the Federal Capital is in Trinidad. Prior to the Federation the Mudie Commission visited the area to advise on the island best suited for the Capital. Barbados was first choice, followed by Jamaica and Trinidad. The Commission made some adverse comments about politics and standards of public life in Trinidad, which caused a good deal of acrimony at the time. In the event, that colony was chosen by local decision as the seat of the Federation. The most favoured site, there, for the capital buildings is still leased to the United States under a war-time agreement for American bases in the Caribbean. So, for the present, the Federal Government is accommodated in temporary quarters in Port-of-Spain.

The people are chiefly of African, East Indian and European descent; with several thousand Chinese in Trinidad and Jamaica. The Africans are directly descended from the slaves brought from the Guinea Coast. Following the abolition of slavery in the early nineteenth century there was a large immigration of indentured labourers from India; their descendants are to be found today mostly in Trinidad and in British Guiana.

Most of the islands are mountainous and of volcanic origin; Antigua and Barbados, being mainly of coral limestone and low-lying, are the exception. The climate throughout is tropical, but it is tempered by trade winds; temperatures average between 75° and 85° Fahrenheit and the range of rainfall in a year can be as low as 30 inches and as high as 200 inches. Hurricanes are not uncommon and there are occasional earthquakes. The hurricane season lasts from June to November, during which period three hurricanes on an average pass over some part of the Caribbean. Risk of serious damage is not very great where buildings are well constructed. A contributory factor to collapse, especially in wooden buildings, is the white ant (or termite), which infests and weakens many timbers commonly used. Considering the amount of timber used, it is surprising how frequently preventive measures are ignored or neglected. If the climate of the Caribbean is kinder than in some other parts of the tropics, the wise designer will still pay heed to problems of ventilation, solar radiation, rain penetration, corrosion, and infestation of materials.

The economy of the West Indies is largely agricultural, the main crops being sugar, bananas and citrus; but minerals – oil and bauxite – and some secondary industries provide valuable additional exports. In a region blest with some of the finest beaches in the world, it is not surprising that the tourist industry is developing rapidly. In 1958, for example, more than 170,000 holidaymakers came to Jamaica, the majority from USA and Canada. In the same year, however, 17,000 West Indians left their native lands to seek their fortunes elsewhere – many in Great Britain.

The population of the West Indies will double itself in forty years or less if the present rate of increase is maintained. This places a severe strain on the slender resources, both from home or abroad, which are available to the region. The first call on these resources is for the general improvement of the economy, but this means that social services, including much-needed housing and health services, must come second. The rate of new house-building is far behind what is needed to remedy overcrowding and obsolescence and to provide for the increasing population. Barbados provides a good illustration of the difficulties. Here the population increases at two per cent per annum. The most optimistic estimate of the rise in the national income during the next generation is that the rate will not exceed one-half per cent per annum. Here is a country with a permanently limited income and a rapidly rising population. One cannot escape the conclusion that some parts, at least, of the West Indies are over-populated. While new harbours, industrial development, education, health and housing improvements are very desirable, nothing Governments can do is comparable in importance with success in arresting the increase of the population.

Of the settlements or architecture of the indigenous Caribs, nothing remains today. What may still be seen, however, are several fair examples of an imported Georgian vernacular, especially in the plantation houses of Barbados and Jamaica. Pierre Labat visited Bridgetown in 1675 – twenty-five years after a serious fire and a hurricane. But already he found 'solid buildings, handsome streets, and warehouses filled with every kind of merchandise; the plantation houses well ventilated, plentifully supplied with glazed windows, well planned and commodious'. He noted that 'People of distinction have live partridges, which they keep in coops . . . one can say that no people exist, who spend more, or who go to greater lengths, to have all that is rarest and best from foreign lands even the most distant. Their houses are well stocked with every kind of wine and liqueur and they are delighted if their guests are hard put to it to find their way home.'

The fine 'Great' houses of Jamaica appeared less impressive to one visitor – Charles Leslie, who wrote in 1739: 'One is not to look for beauties in architecture here; the public buildings are neat, but not fine . . . the gentlemen's houses are generally built low of one storey'. This tradition of one-storey building has to some extent continued, and what Nikolaus Pevsner says of housing in the Dominions (in his Introduction, on page 15) fairly describes the West Indian urban scene today. 'The standard,' he says, 'is the never ending suburb of bungalows widely spaced in the well-to-do, crammed together in the poorer districts. Never do they make visual sense . . . Modern clichés have been absorbed naturally and vulgarized with disarming success . . . The detached dominates everywhere and that again defeats any attempts at visual planning.' Nor is subtopia missing; overhead cables, crude road signs and blatant advertisements assault the eye. Perhaps the onset of tourism will prove a silent ally in the battle for civic decency.

Since 1946 the West Indies have received an average of £2 million a year through the Colonial Development and Welfare Acts, whose object is 'to assist in any purpose likely to promote the development and resources of any colony, or the welfare of its people'. Whenever possible the colony is asked to make a proportionate contribution – be it as little as five per cent or as much as fifty per cent – and all but the poorest have taken the residual recurrent charges on to the local budget. The greater part of these funds has been devoted to education and agriculture, with lesser amounts to health services, water-supply, housing and town-planning in that order. Assistance has also come through the Colonial Development Corporation, which has invested £8 million in the Caribbean since 1948. Its chief stakes are a timber mill in British Guiana, a cement factory in Trinidad and, more recently, a chemical plant and houses for the middle classes in Jamaica. These two external sources of finance, together with local sources, have stimulated a considerable variety of building projects which have called for the services of architects.

Before the war very few architects practised in the West Indies; now several practices have been established – some local, others as branches of firms in Britain. Ancillary services such as those of structural and mechanical engineers and quantity surveyors have also established themselves.

There are as yet no facilities for professional training in architecture, engineering or planning in the West Indies; those seeking it must go to North America, or to the United Kingdom. An engineering faculty is now under consideration at the University College in Jamaica, but the prospects of a faculty for architecture seem remote. Four years ago a mission studied the needs for technical training in the West Indies. It was suggested that the need for architects over the next ten years would be less than 30 qualified men with about 160 assistants; it was also recommended that a large number of supervisors and skilled men would be required for the building industry. These estimates look a little out of scale with what was suggested in the field of engineering – admitting that many of these would be absorbed in the sugar and oil industries. It was suggested that there was a need of 140 civil and structural, 96 mechanical and 56 electrical engineers, plus 900 assistants. Such estimates are not easy to make. It is generally agreed that there is a great need for more training facilities for the building industry; technical schools now under erection in Jamaica and Trinidad will help.

As elsewhere in the Commonwealth there is a growing use of cement, but the present standard of concrete technology cannot be said to be very high. Cement is not the only material produced locally – timber from Guiana and Honduras, asphalt from Trinidad, clay block from Trinidad and Barbados, and gypsum from Jamaica are others. But much has to be imported, and expensive freight rates are reflected in the cost of building. There is no organized building industry as is known here, but several British firms have now established branches in the Caribbean. Wherever they have undertaken a contract – whether for a deep-water harbour, a university college, a hospital, or a luxury hotel – these firms have provided on-the-job training and there has been a marked improvement in the standard of workmanship. Like most people, West Indians will respond to opportunity and encouragement.

WILFRED WOODHOUSE

Trinidad

Office building at San Fernando (architects, Mence and Moore) for the Trinidad and Tobago Electricity Commission. The two storeys of offices, which are one room deep, oversail the ground floor, which is extended in the form of a single-storey wing at the back and contains reception and showroom. Construction is a reinforced concrete frame with rough concrete facing slabs in the end wall and a low basement wall of concrete bricks. The staircase window has horizontal metal louvres. The offices are protected by aluminium and timber sunbreakers.

key
1, general office.
2, balcony.
3, foyers.
4, yard below.
5, stores.
6, tea room.

Above, right: office building, Port-of-Spain
(architects, Prior, Lourenco and Nothnagel).
A three-storey block designed for the later
addition of two more floors. The ground floor
provides showroom space, and this and the office
space above (see plan) has lifts and staircase at
the south-west and north-east corners and
services grouped along the west side to allow
freedom to sub-divide the floor-space as
required. Construction is reinforced concrete.
The south and east façades are protected by
vertical adjustable louvres. The building is
air-conditioned.

Right: Federal House, Port-of-Spain (architects,
Trinidad Works Department; architect in
charge, L. E. Cornialliac). A six-storey office
building originally designed for the Colony
Government but subsequently leased to the new
Federal Authority. It is fully air-conditioned.

Office building, Point Fortin (architects, Prior, Lourenco and Nothnagel). A four-storey air-conditioned block with floor-space designed for maximum flexibility of sub-division by steel partitions. Construction is reinforced concrete with two north-east and south-west façades protected from the sun by vertical light-weight concrete fins and horizontal fixed louvres.

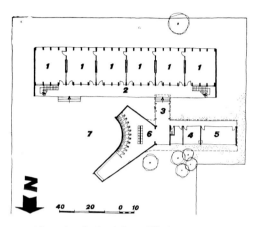

ground floor: boys' school, Port-of-Spain

key: 1, classrooms. 2, corridor. 3, covered way. 4, head teacher. 5, staff room. 6, lavatories. 7, playground.

Above: boys' primary school, Port-of-Spain (architect, Colin Laird). The photograph shows the two-storey classroom block (see plan). Construction is pre-cast reinforced concrete frame with pre-fabricated timber cladding units of egg-crate form on the north side to protect the classroom corridor from north-easterly driving rain.

Below: the new Government House at St Ann's, Port-of-Spain (architects, Mence and Moore), required because the old one is now occupied by the Federal Governor-General. The accommodation is that of a large residence with provision for guests (including, on occasion, Royalty) and for large-scale entertaining. Construction is reinforced concrete with pipe columns and walls of concrete bricks.

Above: office and store building, Port-of-Spain (architects, W. H. Watkins and Partners): the tallest building in Trinidad, 106 ft. high. The sales area occupies the general and first floors, which are connected by escalators. Above are four floors of lettable office space and on the top floor a caretaker's flat and eleven luxury apartments with views south and west to the Gulf of Paria, and north to the mountains. The whole building is air-conditioned. The main façades have continuous curtain-wall glazing, protected against glare by fixed vertical aluminium louvres.

Fire services headquarters, Port-of-Spain
(architects, Mence and Moore), with the
usual accommodation for appliances and
watch-rooms and dormitories above and in
mezzanines at the sides. It has a reinforced
concrete frame and timber floors. Anti-glare
glass is used either side of the entrance.

Office building, Port-of-Spain, for the Cocoa
Board (architects, Mence and Moore): a
reinforced concrete structure of 20 ft. span
with a 10 ft. cantilever either side. Walls are
metal windows and concrete blocks. The roof
is timber.

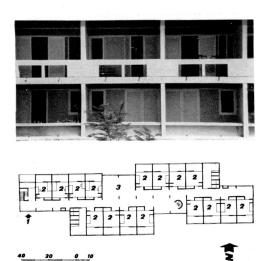

40 20 0 10

ground floor: students' quarters, St Augustine

key: 1, entrance. 2, students' rooms. 3, dining room.

Students' quarters, with dining-room and kitchen, at the Imperial
College of Tropical Agriculture, St Augustine (architect,
R. Llewelyn Davies; supervising architect, Colin Laird). They run
east-west for protection from the sun but are designed to catch
cross-currents of wind, which is mainly easterly. The students'
rooms are in two blocks, each with sixteen rooms to a floor,
arranged in groups of four. Above: the dining-room with open
timber grille and louvred doors to provide through-ventilation.
The structure is reinforced concrete with walls of hollow clay
blocks. Left: the north side.

Staff houses for an oil company, St Joseph
Village (architects, Bolton and Barnstone of
Houston, Texas; supervising architect, Colin
Laird): built to a semi-standard plan used by
the company in various territories. One of the
pair of houses looks inward to a patio; the other
outwards towards open country and the
prevailing breeze. Construction is timber on
stone bases.

Above: Shorelands Hotel, on a promontory overlooking the Gulf of Paria (architect, Anthony C. Lewis). The twelve guest-rooms are in a row on the first floor, each with bathroom and private balcony. The latter have projecting side walls to give privacy. The ground floor has informally planned entrance, reception and staircase opening on to a lounge with an open terrace on the south (sea) side, used for dining, and partly protected by plate-glass screens. Construction is steel columns with reinforced concrete beams. The roof provides clerestory lighting and cross-ventilation to the bedrooms over the top of the corridor. The free-standing ground-floor walls are of local stone.

Below and facing page: a house overlooking the Gulf of Paria (architect, Anthony C. Lewis), on a sloping site of which only a narrow strip was levelled. Main rooms are on the upper floor (see plans) raised on steel columns. The reinforced concrete superstructure has continuous concrete fascias top and bottom. The west elevation (facing page) has both vertical and horizontal louvres. The upper roof is a clerestory with fixed louvres for convection. Cladding is plywood with cedar cover-strips. Ground floor walls are brick.

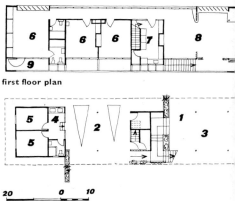

first floor plan

ground floor: house shown below and opposite

20   0   10

key
1, entry.
2, car port.
3, garden porch.
4, laundry.
5, maid.
6, bedrooms.
7, kitchen.
8, living and dining room.
9, balcony

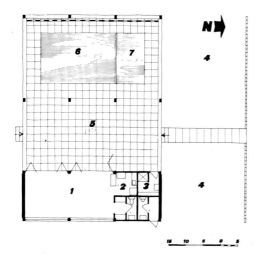

Beach cottage at Bull Bay (architect, Denis G. M. Chalmers), for day and occasional night use. The main room, which can be divided in two by a curtain to serve as living and sleeping room, opens on to a covered patio (see plan) with swimming pool and children's pool. Construction is reinforced concrete with panels of sea-stones from the site. The screen-wall seen in the background in the photograph gives privacy from a main road beyond. The ground between screen and cottage is to be planted as a garden.

key
1, living and sleeping.
2, kitchen.
3, change.
4, gardens.
5, patio.
6, pool.
7, children's pool.

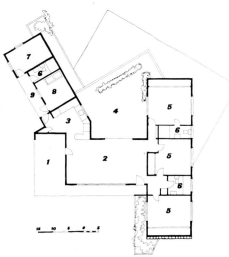

House at St Andrew (architect, Wilson Chong): single-storey, planned round a paved terrace (see plan) with car-port under an extension of the living-room roof. The latter is reinforced concrete, consisting of flat slab and hipped plates. Walls are load-bearing reinforced blocks, plastered. Windows are timber.

plan: house at St Andrew
key: 1, car port. 2, dining and living. 3, kitchen. 4, patio. 5, bedrooms. 6, bathrooms. 7, maid's room. 8, laundry. 9, walkway.

Insurance offices, Kingston (architects, Norman and Dawbarn) for the National Employers' Mutual Insurance Co. and containing additional offices for letting. All but the top floor, which has a folded slab roof protecting the windows, is air-conditioned. The rest of the façade is protected by movable aluminium louvres.

offices at Kingston

key

ground floor plan
1, car park.
2, general office.
3, public waiting space.
4, lobby.
5, lunch room.

first floor plan
1, general office.
2, secretaries.
3, offices.
4, library.
5, vault.
6, public waiting space.
7, reception.

Office building in the business centre of Kingston (architects, Ashwell, Dunn and Associates). It contains general office space and the offices of the architects who designed it. The structure is reinforced concrete with reinforced block infill panels and movable louvres protecting the street front. The roof is insulated against sun by 3 in. of water in an asphalt membrane. The offices are air-conditioned.

Government farm school, between Kingston and Spanish Town (architects, Ashwell, Dunn and Associates): a residential training school for 160 students, on a plateau in the Liguanea Plain. The buildings (laid out in parallel east-west blocks to avoid sun-penetration) are connected by covered ways. The photograph shows the administration and one of the classroom blocks looking eastwards across the garden courtyard. Construction is reinforced concrete with concrete block walls.

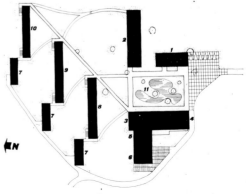

key
1, admin. and library.
2, classrooms and laboratories.
3, dining hall.
4, assembly hall.
5, kitchen.
6, laundry.
7, lavatories and cycle sheds.
8, 9, 10, dormitories.
11, quadrangle.

site plan of farm school

Jamaica

Kingston College of Arts, Science and Technology: the engineering workshops (architects, Norman and Dawbarn). These comprise the second stage of the college, the first having been the conversion of existing buildings into classrooms, dormitories, etc. Further new buildings will follow. The photograph shows the building department workshop, one of three (see plan), each with semi-open work-space in front, and connected by laboratories, staff-rooms, etc. The bins beneath the pierced screen hold materials. Roofs are pre-cast reinforced concrete frames with timber decking.

Hotel at Montego Bay (architects, Ballard, Todd and Snibbe of New York). The one-suite width gives cross-ventilation, avoids internal corridors and gives all rooms a view of the bay. Each suite has a private breakfast-terrace. The ground floor has a restaurant and bar opening on to a swimming pool and open-air dance-floor. The hotel is air-conditioned.

Senior common-room, University College of the West Indies (architects, Norman and Dawbarn): the latest addition to the very extensive group of buildings forming University College, built in 1950–52. It provides recreation and dining-rooms for the senior academic staff and, on the first floor, a library and six visitors' bedrooms. It faces north with views to the Blue Mountains. It has a reinforced concrete frame with concrete block walls.

Terminal building, Montego Bay Airport (architects, Norman and Dawbarn), designed to allow expansion at either end – one end has already had a restaurant added – and to allow a free flow of air through the concourses. The air-side (shown in the photograph) has two-storey offices; the other side is single-storey. The curved roof, which has a pre-cast concrete frame, oversails both sides to shade the windows. The main structural frame is also pre-cast, with wall panels of local stone or concrete blocks.

British Guiana

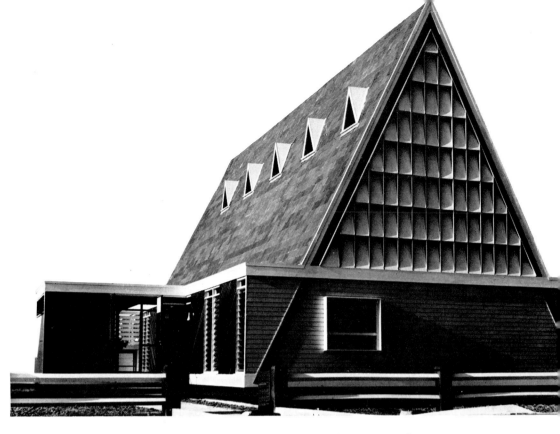

Christian Science Church, British Guiana (architects, Mence and Moore), seating 100 people. It is built wholly of timber: local hardwoods treated against termites. The main roof beams are of greenheart and are unsupported between the ground and the ridge. They are 10 ft. apart and they and the secondary rafters are exposed internally. The roof is covered with grey asbestos slates. Boarded walls are oiled, with fascias painted white. The fixed louvres in the north and south gables are of asbestos in hardwood mullions. The dormer windows have green anti-sun glass.

Leeward Islands

Left: Government offices, St John's, Antigua (architects, Robertson Ward Associates). It also has the offices of the Administrator and the Ministers and staffs. It is one room deep to give cross-ventilation, with access galleries on the lee side. It has a reinforced concrete frame with concrete block walls and steel truss roof covered in asbestos. Balustrading to the galleries is precast concrete.

Below: offices and warehouse, Basseterre, St Kitts (architects, McMorris and Sibley), sited close to the harbour and containing also a retail shop and travel agency. It is in reinforced concrete with walls of local limestone and concrete blocks. On the south-west and north-west elevations (below) aluminium louvred windows are fitted between vertical concrete fins.

Princess Margaret Hospital, Dominica (architect, Michael V. Smith, executive government architect, Windward Islands). Laid out in parallel blocks, running north-south, connected by covered ways (see plan). It was built largely by direct labour. The photograph shows the private patients' block.

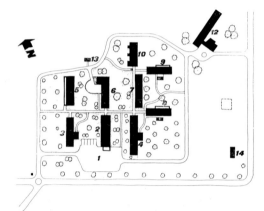

key
1, car parking.
2, admin.
3, medical wards.
4, maternity and children's wards.
5, isolation and observation wards.
6, laundry and kitchen.
7, operating theatre and x-ray.
8, female surgical block.
9, male surgical block.
10, private patients.
12, nurses' hostel.
13, mortuary.
14, matron's quarters.

site plan: hospital at Dominica

Post office, Castries, St Lucia (architect, Michael V. Smith, executive government architect, Windward Islands). It was constructed after a fire which destroyed the whole commercial centre of the town.

Windward Islands

key
1, waiting.
2, doctor's office.
3, treatment room.
4, kitchen.
5, ward pantry.
6, female ward.
7, verandah.
8, covered way.

typical floor plan: Hospital, St. Lucia

Victoria Hospital, St Lucia (architect, Michael V. Smith, executive government architect, Windward Islands): the new T.B. ward, which is the first stage of the rebuilding of a nineteenth-century hospital on a very steep site. The floor above the arcade contains the female ward and the top floor the male ward.

Barbados

Hotel extension, Barbados (architect, Barbara Hill): two blocks with six cabana-type luxury apartments (see plan), serving also to shelter the swimming-pool from the wind. Gardens are reached through the connecting wall. The apartments are staggered in plan to give privacy. The front panels are a grille formed of local clay pots.

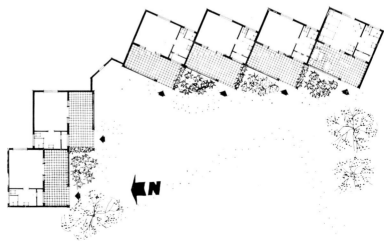

ground floor: hotel extension

School library, Barbados (architect, Anthony C. Lewis):
for Harrison College, but sited in a wooded area away
from the other school buildings. The walls have a saw-tooth
plan to increase the extent of wall-space for shelving.
A clerestory roof increases convection. The photograph
shows the library from the rear, with the reference wing
on the right.

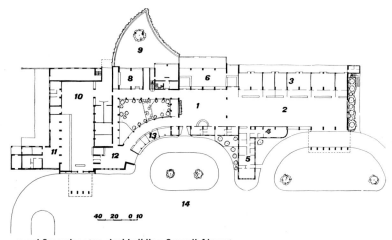

key
1, waiting room.
2, airlines' concourse.
3, airlines' offices.
4, aircrews' room.
5, general office.
6, departure lounge.
8, cocktail lounge.
9, observation patio.
10, customs and immigration.
11, baggage unloading.
12, reception hall.
13, shops.
14, car park.

ground floor plan: terminal building, Seawell Airport

Terminal building, Seawell Airport
(architect, K. J. Tomlin, Director of Public
Works, Barbados), planned round an open
patio (see plan); on the first floor are the
main concourse and restaurant. Walls and
columns are of local coral limestone, with
steel roof covered in asbestos.

India, Pakistan and Ceylon

FOR THE POOR OF ASIA shelter has always been, and still is, a matter of self-help. The peasants of India, Pakistan and Ceylon need but little of it, because most of their lives are spent in the open; but they do need some protection from sun and rain, occasional privacy, and safe storage-places for their belongings. Their urge to beautify and decorate is seldom applied to the whole house, but to essential parts, such as the door or threshold (the Indian housewife decorates the threshold of her house every morning with patterns of rice flour), to images of domestic gods, oil lamps, clay or brass pots and other objects of daily use. The flowers used to adorn the domestic altar and the hair-do of women are significant signs of the need to brighten an incredibly hard and drab life.

The poor man's (and woman's) need for spectacular buildings, as subjects of his day-dreams, was catered for in the past by the houses of his gods with their incredible wealth of figurative decoration, and by the splendour of the palaces of maharajas and emperors. The fact that the architecture of the imperial palaces from the Moguls to the British Viceroys was basically foreign, and that of the maharajas imitated the worst Victorian horrors, did not affect its capacity to satisfy this need.

Independence brought a complete change. Gandhi and his disciples had established an image of a new country that was both romantic (going back to the simple life and self-contained economy of the village, wearing hand-spun and hand-woven cloth) and puritan (prohibition, reduction of top pay-scales, abolition of rajahs, imposition of a luxury tax). The leaders of the new India accepted Lutyens's New Delhi as a convenience, but resented it as an inappropriate setting for the hard-working public servants of a poor country. They prepared five-year plans for a community of responsible citizens and scorned any idea of fobbing off the ruled with *panem et circenses*.

It was in keeping with this general attitude, which prevailed to a lesser degree also in the first years of the new Pakistan and Ceylon, that architectural interest concentrated at first almost exclusively on low-cost housing. The best brains of the three countries were concerned with new towns (India started twelve between 1945 and 1951), prefabrication, village improvement and community development.

Public buildings, instead of being welcomed as opportunities of expressing the aspirations of the new countries, were treated as necessary evils. Confusion reigned as to their shape and style. The 'moderns' wanted to prove that Asians could do as well or better than the West in applying new technologies. The traditionalists advocated a return to historical patterns in the belief that one could, thereby, create something typically Pakistani, Indian or Ceylonese. Many intellectuals thought that attention to climate and the use of local materials would be enough to create a new national style.

It is necessary to understand the Indian background, as well as these post-war currents of emotion and thinking, to appreciate the impact of Le Corbusier's work at Chandigarh. The High Court and Secretariat buildings of the Punjab capital were the urgently needed proof that public buildings in India could be modern, yet different from contemporary work – even by the same architect – elsewhere. That does not mean that they were popular. A public-opinion poll amongst literate Indians (still a minority) would probably produce a strong vote against them. But more important than approval or dislike is the fact that the buildings of Chandigarh were the first examples of post-war architecture that aroused heated discussion throughout the country. Their high costs enhanced rather than diminished their importance as focal points of public interest, and of the day-dreams – if not of the poor Indian masses, at least of a new generation of Indian architects.

After the completion of these Chandigarh buildings we find at various points of the sub-continent architects who, if they do not exactly imitate Le Corbusier, have the courage of their own convictions and try to find their own mode of expression. They are still lonely swallows, but they *are* emerging. Their efforts are helped by the trends of the second and third five-year plans which have gone far towards restoring the balance between village development, on the one side, and industrialization and modern technology, on the other, and have increased confidence in technical progress.

India, Pakistan and Ceylon have strong and highly developed engineering professions. Indians lead in irrigation-engineering and command vast experience in the construction of dams and canals. The architectural profession has developed only in the last four decades, and the number of qualified architects is small – about one per million of inhabitants in India and one per ten million in Pakistan. Practising architects are concentrated mainly in the large cities. Most of the design work in small towns and villages is handled by civil engineers or small builders.

India has five schools of architecture with five-year courses and examinations controlled by a governmental Board of Technical Studies which aims at standards comparable to those in Britain. One Indian school, that of the Indian Institute of Technology at Kharagpur (Bengal), has a Graduate School of Design modelled on that of MIT. Pakistan and Ceylon have no schools of architecture and depend on training abroad; but Pakistan has plans for the establishment of schools at Karachi, Lahore and Dacca, one under Colombo Plan auspices and the other two with the help of the Ford Foundation.

An architect practising in Bombay or Calcutta could in theory command all the materials and equipment available to his colleagues in the West. In practice, he is restricted by shortages of steel (Indian steel production is increasing rapidly, but is still far short of the country's needs), and his choice of panelling and cladding materials and fittings is limited. More and more building materials and components are made in India, but many of the less frequently used items must be imported. The shortage of steel accounts for the almost complete absence of steel-frame construction and the preponderance of concrete. The use of large areas of glass is ruled out by climatic considerations.

Air-conditioning is used more and more in important commercial and public buildings, but is still far too expensive for universal application. In most buildings, the architect must combat severe climatic conditions without it. India, Pakistan and Ceylon include climatic regions of great variety and contrast, ranging from the warm-humid equatorial areas of Western Ceylon, the Malabar Coast and Bengal to the hot-dry desert or near-desert conditions of Rajputana and Sind. Large areas of the sub-continent have Intermediate or Monsoon climates; that is, they are hot and dry for almost two-thirds of the year, and warm and humid for the remainder. The hill-towns of the Himalayas have to cope with severe winters; settlements in Assam and in the Malnad 'boast' of the highest rainfall figures in the world, and some areas such as the Mysore plateau enjoy a pleasant, almost sub-tropical, climate.

Traditional building practices and local materials vary in accordance with the different climates, and these affect contemporary buildings as they have affected those of the past. It is still far too early to discern clearly Indian, Pakistani, or Ceylonese architectural movements. The new countries of Asia need time to develop modern vernaculars of their own, but promising beginnings can be found as the following pages show.

O. H. KOENIGSBERGER

Hotel at Ahmedabad (architect, C. M. Correa). The riverside site slopes steeply
and the entrance driveway takes cars up to first floor level, where the public
lounges, dining-rooms, etc., are placed – see section, right. At the lower level is
a general-purpose public room opening on to the garden and a shopping arcade.
The bedrooms above are planned round an internal garden and a lift and service
core. The base of the building is of exposed brick and the upper part is
plastered white.

The Millowners' Building at Ahmedabad (architect, Le Corbusier). This is an
office building, containing also conference and meeting rooms, for the local
Association of Millowners. It is of exposed reinforced concrete construction and is
shown in the photograph from across the Sabarnati River.

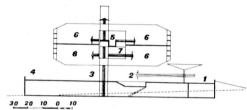

section through hotel at Ahmedabad

key: 1, drive. 2, entrance. 3, lounge. 4, terrace. 5, bridge.
6, rooms. 7, garden.

The High Court at Chandigarh, the new capital of
East Punjab, of which Le Corbusier is the planner as
well as being the architect of this and other public
buildings. The High Court forms one of a group of
buildings, all of fully exposed reinforced concrete, raised
up above the rest of the city on what is known as the
capitol, at the northern end of the main axis. Above: the
southern side, seen across an artificial pool.

The Secretariat, Chandigarh (architect, Le Corbusier).
It stands on the capitol at the northern end of the city,
but at the opposite side from the High Court (see
preceding page), from the roof of which this photograph
is taken, looking north-west. Eventually the parliament
building will be between them. It accommodates 3,000
employees and is divided vertically by a series of expansion
joints into six ministerial blocks, each consisting of office-
space either side of a central corridor. The wall with
small apertures to the left of the centre of the façade is
that of an enclosed ramp standing out at an angle and
serving all floors. The section further to the right, with
a changing pattern of brise-soleil, is that of the
Ministers' offices. The roof-top structures house
club-rooms, etc.

key
1. entrance to main block.
2. technological block.
3. future extensions.
4. tower.
5. cooling pond.
6. car park.
7. auditorium.

site plan: Electronics Research Institute

Above: the Central Electronics Research Institute, Pilani, Rajasthan Province (architects, Kanvinde and Rai), one of a chain of national research laboratories. The buildings, on a flat site, are in three groups (see plan), the main group, housing the quieter activities (centre of photograph), including offices, research laboratories, museum and library; a lecture theatre and cafeteria group (on the right behind the tower), and a technological group containing workshops, etc. (on the left). The tower, which is linked to the main buildings by a bridge, is for cosmic ray research. The structure is a reinforced concrete frame with brick infill walls. Vertical adjustable asbestos louvres give sun-protection.

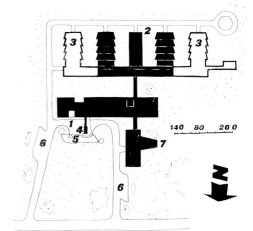

Left: Nalini Banker house, Ahmedabad (architects, Vastu-Shilpa; partner in charge, Balkrishna V. Doshi): a single-storey, two-bedroom house, rectangular in plan with a central courtyard open on one side. The photograph shows the south end, with recessed porch leading straight into the living-room and, on the left, the two corner windows of the main bedroom. Construction is reinforced concrete with brick infill.

Above: housing at Chandigarh, East Punjab (architect, E. Maxwell Fry). Part of a terrace of one of the numerous standardized house-types evolved for the residential quarters of the city by Maxwell Fry, Jane Drew and Pierre Jeanneret, working under Le Corbusier's planning control. This two-storey type has three bedrooms, two sitting-rooms and a screened sleeping-terrace on the roof.

Above (right): Shodhan house, Ahmedabad (architect, Le Corbusier): in exposed concrete showing the imprint of timber shuttering, except on the roof-soffit where the surface is smooth, derived from sheet-metal shuttering, and brightly coloured. Main living-rooms, etc., are half-way up. This floor, and the floor below, are reached by an internal ramp.

Above: Chinubhai House, Ahmedabad (architects, Vastu-Shilpa): a three-storey house with exposed reinforced concrete frame incorporating cantilevered slabs forming balconies. The small amount of infill walling is of narrow red bricks laid with straight joints.

Above: staff houses for the Physical Research Laboratory, Ahmedabad (architects, Vastu-Shilpa; partner in charge, Balkrishna V. Doshi). One of a series of dwelling types evolved for research organizations. Construction is wholly brick, including the vaulted roofs. Windows are unglazed, and have either wooden shutters or metal louvres. The 4-in. slit under the vault has only flywire. (See plan, left.)

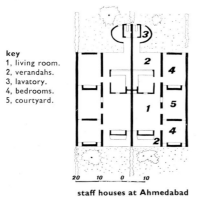

key
1, living room.
2, verandahs.
3, lavatory.
4, bedrooms.
5, courtyard.

20 10 0 10

staff houses at Ahmedabad

Pakistan

Headquarters, Karachi, of the Pakistan Boy Scouts Association (architects, Taj-ud-Din M. Bhamani & Co.). The building is at Queen's Road, near the sea. It has a floor area of 10,000 sq. ft. and is designed to accommodate rallies, meetings and other functions and to house visiting scouts from other countries. The structure is a reinforced concrete frame with concrete block panel walls and concrete grilles where rooms need screening from the sun.

Columbus Hotel, Karachi (architects, Taj-ud-Din M. Bhamani & Co.). It is on the main Clifton Road and contains forty bedrooms plus lounge, dining-room and bar. All rooms face towards the westerly breeze and have a distant view of the sea. The whole building, which is of reinforced concrete construction, is air-conditioned.

Bank offices, Karachi (architects, Taj-ud-Din M. Bhamani & Co.). Situated at the junction of Kingsway and Strachan Road, the building houses the foreign exchange branch of the State Bank of Pakistan. Construction is reinforced concrete with flat slab floors and panel walls and vertical and horizontal sun-screens.

Left: Beach Hotel, Karachi (architect, D. H. Daruvala). The photograph shows the ground-floor banqueting rooms, with lounges, etc. raised above it and walled almost wholly in glass to give a panoramic view over the sea.

Left: flats at Karachi (architect, D. H. Daruvala) for the Pakistan Industrial Development Corporation. Construction is in reinforced concrete. The whole of the ground floor area is left open, owing to the dampness of the site, and is used as a children's play-space.

Below: public library, Dacca (architect, Muzharul Islam). It is of reinforced concrete construction and the reading-room wing on the far side has a vaulted roof of shell concrete. Also in Dacca (capital of East Pakistan) is a Government institute of arts by the same architect.

Left, art gallery, Karachi (architects, Taj-ud-Din M. Bhamani & Co.). In a prominent position at the junction of Ingle Road and Strachan Road, it is raised on columns so that its surrounding garden continues beneath the building, and is planned so that its two galleries are lit from north and south, avoiding easterly and westerly sun but getting the benefit of the south-westerly breeze. The ground floor contains a café as well as the garden terrace. On the first and second floors are the two galleries (each with 24 alcoves), and on the top floor the curator's office, a music-room and committee-rooms. The upper floors are reached by a ramp, placed behind the open grilles on the right of the picture. A future extension will include an assembly hall.

Above: office building, Lahore (architects, Terry and Black), which has been built for the West Pakistan Road Transport Board. There are shops on the ground floor of the front wing facing the street, and penthouse flats on the third floor. It was one of the first reinforced concrete-frame buildings in Lahore and has brick cladding. The north façade (shown here) has vertical sun-screens for use against the late evening summer sun; on the south façade there are both vertical and horizontal sun-screens.

Below: shops and flats at Peshawar (architects, Terry and Black) which are sited opposite the brick ramparts of Peshawar Fort. The building is planned as two wings at right-angles to each other, each with a street frontage. In the wing facing west the flats have verandahs screened by concrete grilles (the corner verandah can be seen in the picture); the other frontage (shown here) tries to maintain the small-scale variety of incident, traditional to Peshawar street architecture, in the design of the loggia openings.

House at Colombo (architect, Minnette de Silva). Built in reinforced concrete round a garden court. A car-port is under the overhanging first floor; to the left is the court-yard. The traditional-shaped gable-vents also serve as niches for oil lamps at festivals. Below: looking through the living-room into the garden; a wooden trellis, on left, separates off the courtyard.

The garden front of a house at Kandy (architect, Minnette de Silva). The different sections of the house change level to follow the slope of the ground. Construction is reinforced concrete and timber.

Malaya

THE FEDERATION OF MALAYAN STATES occupies that thin limb which the Asian continent throws out in a south-easterly direction, very nearly touching the Equator, known geographically as the Malacca Peninsula. It is virtually an island, the smallest of the Sunda Archipelago isles which include Sumatra and Borneo. Architecturally it possesses but thin local traditions and, consequently, few viable local prototypes of buildings. At the same time, it lies across the main road of world trade and is, therefore, immeasurably more advanced and Westernized than its neighbours.

Half the present population consists of recent immigrants: Chinese, Indians, Europeans. Of these, the Chinese form by far the largest, and also the most conspicuous, element. The other half, though having a much older birthright in the peninsula, is likewise not indigenous, for the Malays, too, are immigrants. The truly native element is represented by the remnants of tribal population living in the hills of the less Westernized among the Malayan states. As a subject for study, in particular for their ways of living in houses and building them, they are full of interest; as a community in the Federation they are practically without influence.

A near-island, then, and a new country. Its population of over five million – rapidly increasing – is living on the still flourishing industries of tin-mining and rubber-growing. It has recently achieved independence, as a federal monarchy remaining in the Commonwealth, and is very much a country on the move. Kuala Lumpur, the capital, at present a city of about 450,000 inhabitants, is expected to pass the million mark within the next twenty-five years. Its face is changing almost monthly. It has the outcrop of miniature skyscrapers which is so typical of up-and-coming places – with the traffic problems following in their wake. It has many cinemas, some of them very smart indeed. You can hear concerts and plays there; it has its Radio Malaya; it has libraries, high schools; even a division of the University of Malaya is moving up from Singapore. Recently a grand, indeed a grandiloquent, avenue has been completed which was meant to lead to the 'diplomatic enclave', a piece of high ground in the rubber hills west of the town where every embassy was supposed to build its seat. This may never happen; but something is bound to happen on those newly developed sites. There is no lack of movement, if it is not always in the best direction.

This optimism is based upon one thing mainly: the talent and enthusiasm to be found in both the large communities, Malay and Chinese. If one remembers that architecture, as the West understands it at present, town-planning and housing are all in Malaya very new crafts and sciences indeed, the results visible already are remarkable, and it is not surprising that there are not yet any major architectural achievements to show. Compared with the architecture of those tropical countries which have recently moved into the very focus of the new architecture, recent Malayan buildings can at best be called responsible and at worst frankly amusing.

Malaya, at present, has much in common with certain other newly independent countries in the Commonwealth which are trying to shape a progressive and, at the same time, distinctive nation. This implies that it looks, in architecture – as in other things – towards Europe and, at the same time, tries to find a short cut towards a Malayan architecture. But while elsewhere Europe still means, mainly, Britain the colonizer, in Malaya it means Britain, America, Australia and recently Germany. Chinese Malays and Indians are much less dependent upon the one source of Western influence. They themselves represent ancient civilizations; and while European civilization (in the wide sense, including oversea Europeanized countries) seems as inevitable here as it would seem to be elsewhere, Chinese and Malays do exercise a choice. They have been meeting Europeans on equal terms since long before Independence, they have been mixing socially, they have been working together in business, in administration, in schools; and there, also, on equal terms.

This greater maturity brings with it its own problems. At present, every foreign plant is being put into the architectural soil of the Federation: and it grows. Nobody can say that the designs made by the many young Chinese architects trained oversea – mostly in Melbourne – are less foreign than the designs of the British architects still guiding the building effort of the Public Works Department, many of the larger municipalities and such public utility bodies as the Central Electricity Board. It may seem paradoxical, but it is largely true that the local British architect cares more about a tropical architecture – and certainly no less about a 'Malayan' one – than his Asian colleague. He is also the one who most vigorously campaigns for the use of the local building material, timber, and who devotes a loving interest to the study of traditional Malay and tribal houses. The situation, at times, recalls that ancient cartoon where Serenissimus, visiting a village in his principality, is shown in local garb while the village notables receive him dressed in their towny best.

All recognize, however, that the way towards a suitable tropical architecture for this country – which, in time, may or may not develop into a Malayan architecture – can only be by way of research and the building up of local training. In both fields, the first steps are already being taken; in particular, the training of Malayan architects within the Federation has recently begun.

A power for good, in the development of a responsible architecture, is the Public Works Department. This has only become so recently, and it may not yet be the case in certain outstations where they have not yet a State Architect but an engineer looking after building design. Also, the type of PWD house for the occupation of Government officers, though well planned, is, with one exception, poorly designed and poorly executed. The exception is a type developed by a young architect; and the change which has come about in the work of the PWD is mainly due to young architects who have had to design quite large buildings. They react to this opportunity by taking an active interest in the country which gives it to them. Some of them have traversed Malaya on foot, sleeping in Malay houses and studying them; nearly all interest themselves in the training of architects locally and one, Norman Lehey, has given up his post in PWD to take up full-time teaching at the Technical College.

But the most significant contribution of PWD to the hoped-for future architecture of Malaya is found in its work, some of which is shown on the following pages. Its design may be 'international' or 'European' – it is difficult to see how it could be anything else – but it is sober, restrained and thoughtful. The buildings are, on the whole, well planned and (which is possibly even more important) well detailed; last, but not least, it shows a tendency towards a correct tropical – if not actually a Malayan – way of building. Among practising local architects, there are also some who are moving in the same direction, but the conditions prevailing in a large public office, which is its own client, are more favourable to experiment.

Another organization with a large and enterprising programme is the Housing Trust, which was established in 1950 and is now working under the Ministry of the Interior. The gigantic nature of the task it has to tackle is indicated by the following extract from a statement issued by the Trust in November, 1959:

'From the 1957 census it is found that there are approximately 70,000 families living in squatter huts in urban areas, that a further 45,000 families are living as sub-tenants, mostly in one room, and that in order to house the annual increase in the population, which amounts to 3 per cent, a further 25,000 houses will be needed every year. This means that at least 120,000 houses are needed now to provide homes for badly housed families, in addition to the 25,000 required each year. Although these figures may not seem large to Western eyes, it should be remembered that the total of households in the Federation is 1,258,561.'

The figures are, indeed, desperately large and out of all proportion to funds available. The Housing Trust has mainly, since 1953 when its full staff was appointed, built low-cost houses for re-sale in outlying parts of towns and in the 'new town' of Petaling Jaya. More recently, after the fire of 1956, it has built, jointly with the municipality, two major housing schemes, including flats and shops, in the heart of Kuala Lumpur; more recently still, it is developing minimum types of houses and, in conjunction with the Forestry Department of the Government, it is designing timber houses which can be mainly built by the purchaser himself, and helping the purchaser to acquire them.

Finally, something must be said about one-family private houses, because these are the playground of Malaya's young architecture. Kuala Lumpur, which is marvellously situated at the foot of the central chain of hills – a kind of Malayan Apennines rising to over 6,500 feet, densely covered with jungle – is surrounded by lower hills, and these are now being covered with the new garden suburbs. The most popular is Kenny Hill, overlooking the high chains and their rocky cave-riddled foothills. The houses here and in similar places are often amusing, endearing even, and brimming with the newest and the best from everywhere.

Some of their architects are not fully qualified, but shelter behind the signature of a qualified friend; others are by qualified architects, mostly with Australian degrees, the majority Chinese. These architects are full of zest, ready at any moment to fire all their guns at once; and they are not necessarily their own guns either: butterfly roofs or other roofing oddities, V-shaped supports, all sorts of concrete grilles, louvres, fins, eccentric canopies, framed windows deeply boxed out, etc. Every house must show as many building materials as is feasible: rubble, brick and, recently, timber; also ornamental grilles and, should any surface remain unadorned, abstract murals. Often, however, the houses are very well planned, including nearly always a double-height living space with rooms leading off at different levels. One architect proudly proclaimed that his house, on a steep slope – they are nearly all slope-houses – had seven levels. The designers say that every hooded window, ornamental concrete grille and broken-up roof has been designed 'to suit the climate,' the owners believe it and call their house cool – which quite often it is on these windswept slopes – and it would be unfair not to admit that those features, before they became mere decoration, had meaning as protection against sun and glare; and this includes strong colours which are always agreeable here.

However, the predominance of such designs has been challenged in recent years, and all sorts of houses are now going up, from the gaily vulgar to 'architects' austere', with the majority finding themselves a shelf somewhere between those extremes. Even more promising, there begin to appear more and more houses whose designers seem to have given thought to the climate and to deal with it in a less haphazard way.

JULIUS POSENER

196

Malaya

Flats at Kuala Lumpur (architects, R. H. H. Davis, chief architect, Federation of Malaya Housing Trust, and Vernon Z. Newcombe); part of a large housing scheme. A general view of the flats, and a plan, are given on the next page. The external façades are enlivened by projecting groups of two or three windows as triangular bays. The windows are shuttered, with a hooded top section for permanent ventilation. Groups of the shutters are painted in different colours: yellow, grey, white and olive green, and the walls behind the access galleries on the other side of the building (which can be seen in the left background of the illustration on the next page) are painted a dark red.

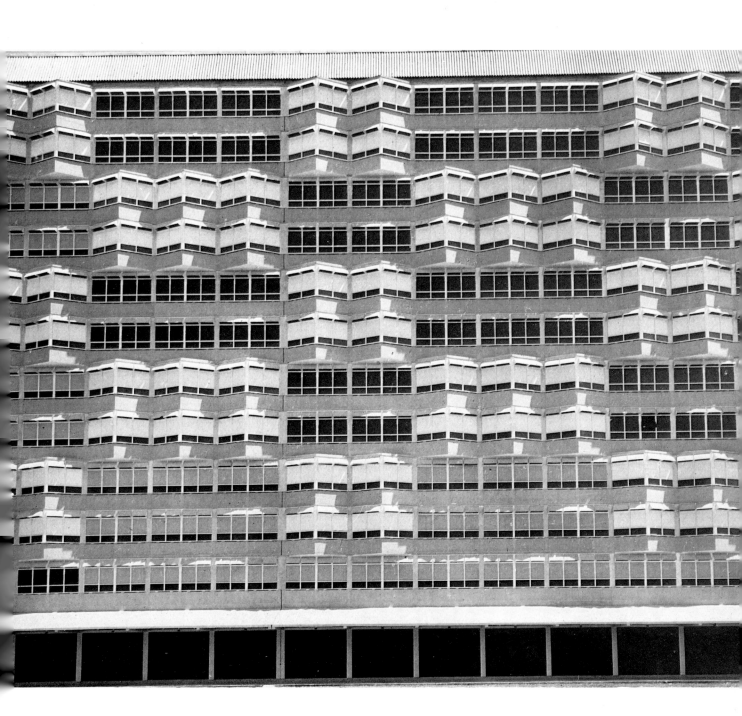

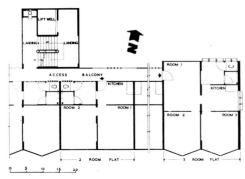

plan of typical flats.

Flats at Kuala Lumpur (architects, R. H. H. Davis, chief architect Federation of Malaya Housing Trust, and Vernon Z. Newcombe) – see façade-detail on the preceding page, seen from the approach to Kuala Lumpur down Batu Road. The flats are part of a large housing scheme for really poor people (see plan on left). There are 280 flats in all. The twelve-storey block illustrated is one of two separated by a courtyard. The access balconies face inwards, so that the flats themselves face northward in one block and southward in the other block – thus having almost identical aspects, since Kuala Lumpur is only three degrees north of the equator. The access balconies can be seen in the portion of the block appearing in the background in the illustration. Construction is a reinforced concrete box-frame with cantilevered galleries.

Offices and courthouse at Ipoh, for the Department of Religious Affairs and Malay Custom (architect, P. G. Morley, Public Works Department, Perak) – see plan below. The office building (right of photograph) has a mezzanine floor at either end of a V-shaped roof which slopes inwards to a reinforced concrete gutter wide enough for a cleaner to walk along it. Both buildings have reinforced concrete portal frames of diminishing height; the lower parts of the walls are composed of glazed steel doors pivoted top and bottom, and the upper part of wooden frames with fixed glass louvres for permanent ventilation.

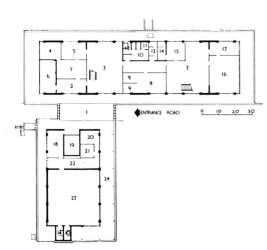

key

1, porch.	12, bath.
2, foyer.	13, president's lavatory.
3, general office.	14, women's lavatory.
4, mufti and katib.	15, female clerks.
5, super kathis.	16, president.
6, canteen.	17, secretary.
7, library.	18, appeal committee.
8, missionary.	19, witnesses.
9, fund section.	20, 21, offices.
10, men's lavatory.	22, clerk and registrar.
11, store.	23, appeal court.
	24, covered way.

Government offices at Petaling Jaya, the site of a new satellite town planned near Kuala Lumpur (architect, P. S. Merer, succeeded by Howard Ashley, Public Works Department). The main building – a six-storey block – runs north and south. Linked to it by a covered way are a square two-storey chemical research building and a canteen – see plan below. The office block is of reinforced concrete with a 12-ft. cantilever on the long sides. These have continuous windows protected by a concrete grille 18 in. in front. The short sides have vertical concrete fins to protect the staircase and lavatory windows. The walls are grey mosaic and the window-panels red. The building is air-conditioned.

key
1, office entrance.
2, air-conditioning plant.
3, air-conditioning stores.
4, post office.
5, car port.
6, secondary entrance.
7, canteen.
8, laboratory block entrance and offices.
9, laboratories.

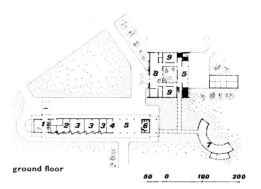

ground floor

Fire Station at Kota Bharu (architect, Norman G. Lehey, Public Works Department, Kelantan). The two-storey main block, facing west, contains the appliances, workshops and duty-rooms on the ground floor and living-quarters over. Behind is a single-storey instruction and office wing, enclosing a parade and training ground. The living quarters are screened by vertical pre-cast concrete fins, with reinforced concrete beams top and bottom.

Arts Building, University of Malaya, Kuala Lumpur – the main body of the university being at Singapore (architect, William Chen of Palmer and Turner). The main four-storey block with open ground floor has three lecture-halls behind (on the right in the photograph) linked by covered ways. Concrete grilles protect the windows from the sun.

Bank and offices, Kuala Lumpur (architects, Booty, Edwards and Partners): a temporary building to serve between the demolition of the old premises of the Mercantile Bank and the erection of new ones by the same architects. It occupies an awkward triangular corner site in Mountbatten Road, in the business centre. The office floors are reached by a circular staircase from the ground-floor bank. The building is concrete-framed with exposed diagrid floor-slabs and fixed vertical fins to protect the office windows. It is air-conditioned.

Terminal Building, Kuala Lumpur Airport (architect, P. S. Merer, Public Works Department). Concourse, restaurant, passenger controls and customs are on the ground floor, with offices and a viewing lounge above. At the west end (on the left of the photograph) is another single-storey lounge. The control tower was originally intended to be above the main staircase (right of photograph). The windows are protected by vertical aluminium fins inserted between the members of a continuous concrete frame. The staircase has a blue ceramic grille.

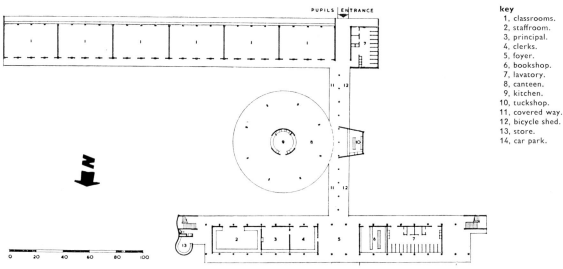

PUPILS | ENTRANCE

key
1, classrooms.
2, staffroom.
3, principal.
4, clerks.
5, foyer.
6, bookshop.
7, lavatory.
8, canteen.
9, kitchen.
10, tuckshop.
11, covered way.
12, bicycle shed.
13, store.
14, car park.

0   20   40   60   80   100

Girls' School, Penang (architect, W. I.
Shipley, Public Works Department, Penang).
It consists of a three-storey classroom block
with staffrooms on the ground floor (photograph
on left), a single-storey classroom block
and a circular canteen and tuckshop (above).
The buildings are connected by covered
ways and are of reinforced concrete. Windows
are metal, with coloured glass panels below,
backed by built-in furniture.

A pair of houses at Kuala Lumpur (architects, Booty, Edwards and Partners). These are staff houses for the Mercantile Bank. They are entered from a terrace at first-floor level, the ground floor being occupied by garages and existing only at the front owing to the steeply sloping site. The verandah which covers the whole façade is closed-in in the centre by a concrete grille to form a porch and is sub-divided vertically to give privacy to the second-floor balconies.

Police-station and district headquarters, Balik Pulau (architect, W. I. Shipley, Public Works Department, Penang). A group comprising a two-storey building (shown in photograph) containing police-station, cells and offices, and single-storey canteen and recreation block, garage block and fire station. The two-storey block is reinforced concrete with window panels of yellow enamelled sheet metal.

Singapore

ANY ASSESSMENT OF RECENT ARCHITECTURE in Singapore must be made against the background of a fine traditional Palladian idiom, originating in England and exported to India by the East India Company and thence to Singapore when that colony was founded in 1819. The military engineer-officers and architects of the British Army in India, often using pattern-books of the classical orders, were quick to see how adaptable the Doric and Tuscan orders were to tropical use. So was evolved what might be called the colonial classic style, with its dignified white façades, buildings one room deep for free air movement, its wide verandahs and footways behind the colonnades, giving shade and protection to the inner walls and sensible louvred openings and hooded windows.

This splendid tradition deserves emphasis because the local understanding of climate upon which it was based has since been lost sight of. Present work shows a good deal of insincerity in design, and while the new tropical architecture of the central Americas and other low latitude territories is entering a brilliant and vital phase, the architects of Singapore seem not to have comprehended the fundamentals of the new approach, and have been content to apply the outward forms and elements of the modern movement indiscriminately to their work. We see irritating architectural mannerisms repeatedly used, together with such structural forms as the hyperbolic paraboloid simply because the architect felt he was being 'modern' in using them. There is no recognizable evolution from the past of a contemporary local style. In fact, a sharp break has been made with the past, which is perhaps understandable in a place where influences from East and West converge. Singapore is an entrepôt city through which is channelled the materials and ideas of the world, and it is not surprising that the superficialities of an international style should be seized on by this rapidly expanding and cosmopolitan city as an expression of its ambitions.

New European and American materials are everywhere in evidence. The ease with which they are obtained has resulted in the use of all the standard building elements manufactured in those countries, so that the office block recently completed on Collyer Quay, Singapore, for instance, would not look out of place in London or New York. The traditional materials were local bricks laid and plastered in lime and sand and roofs covered with palm thatch or locally made Chinese tiles, which gave great character to the building. The latter, unfortunately, have given way to the Marseille pattern tile. Bricks and cement blocks are manufactured in Singapore, cement and steel being imported. Excellent timber from Malaya is available and Chinese labour is capable of a high standard of workmanship.

Life in low latitude territories where the climate is hot and humid is only tolerable when buildings are designed to keep people cool. That is why the early buildings were so successful. In Singapore there is considerable thermal discomfort. Winds which are light and variable cannot be counted on to keep one cool. Air temperatures of 84°, with a relative humidity of 85 per cent, are of common occurrence. Design considerations should, therefore, provide for free air-movement to prevent the inside temperature rising above the shade temperature. This process is defeated if the air is allowed to move across hot surfaces like the tops of concrete roofs and areas of paving, thereby heating it up before it enters the building. Large openings are needed to give the greatest benefit on those days when there is only a slight breeze. Buildings should be orientated to take advantage of the prevailing winds and to minimize the effect of the sun, which is most intense on the east and west. It is desirable to expose as little wall surface as possible to these points of the compass, and to protect exposed walls by shading and projections. All openings must have protection from the sun, glare and driving rain in the form of canopies, verandahs and various kinds of louvred sun-breaker. The latter offer some degree of protection at the same time as admitting air. Permanent openings are necessary at ceiling and floor level and the roof space should be well ventilated and insulated. All surfaces should be light in colour to reduce the transmission of heat into the building.

These are stringent requirements, and the success of the designs have depended on the degree to which the architect has satisfied them. Unfortunately they are often neglected or, if considered, misapplied. The sun-breaker, for instance, is used in a clumsy and unscientific way – the device is not fully understood. From the point of view of the people who have to live and work in these buildings, there is much cause for complaint. Large areas of glass are exposed to the sun, thereby intensifying heat and glare, and subsequent steps have to be taken to combat this with blinds, hoods, fans, air-conditioning and other means. The need to allow for maximum air movement is overlooked, as can be seen by the absence of permanent ventilation at ceiling and floor level and by the use of fenestration copied from European examples and therefore unsuitable for the tropics.

There are, however, a few recent examples of work that redeem this sombre picture, and does show that there is some basic thinking about the fundamentals of good architecture, but there is little evidence of real understanding of the exciting trends elsewhere. The poverty of design cannot be for want of stimulus from nature. What more could an architect demand as a setting for his buildings than the brilliant sunshine giving heavy, luminous shadows and the bright colours and lush, green vegetation? Those public authorities that are engaged in building, such as the Singapore Improvement Trust, the Public Works Department and the Services have a great opportunity and responsibility to further the interests of good architecture because they carry out such a large proportion of the total work. In the field of private work, more and more will be executed by Asian architects who have been trained in the traditions of the West. There are outstanding exceptions, but generally their approach is naïve. There is no reason, however, why they should not in due course bring the freshness to their solutions that can be seen in Japan today.

To bring about an improvement in the standard of design, architectural education of a liberal kind will have to be instituted as a first step. Some progress in this direction had already been made, but the new self-governing state has suppressed this to the detriment of architectural progress. It is to be hoped that the folly of this step will soon be realized. Ultimately, it is the integrity and vision of the architect and his response to the conditions for which he is designing which will enable modern Singapore architecture to bring about a significant contribution to the contemporary scene.

LINCOLN PAGE

Above: flats for senior Government officers (architect, M. J. Cotton, Public Works Department). They have either two or three bedrooms, with lift and staircase access. The open part of the ground floor provides a children's covered play-space. Construction is in reinforced concrete.

Below: housing on the Princess Estate, Queenstown (architect, P. R. Davison, Singapore Improvement Trust): planned in four-storey blocks with variety given to the façades by changes in the colour and texture of walls and window-shutters – load-bearing cross-wall construction, using hollow blocks for thermal insulation.

Left: housing at Queenstown (architect, Lincoln Page, Singapore Improvement Trust). The building has balcony access with semi-enclosed stair at each end. The recessed panels on the façade (which are coloured deep blue) arise from the variation in room-depth required by bathrooms and kitchens. These are opposite-handed on alternate floors to give the chequer effect.

Left (below): housing at Tiong Bahru (architect, Lincoln Page, Singapore Improvement Trust). There are six flats to each stair and shops on the ground floor. Construction is a reinforced concrete frame with cement-block infill walls, rendered brick-red on the main façade with surrounds in white.

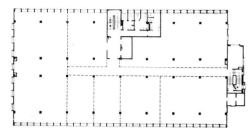

plan of office building

Below: office building (architects, van Sitteren and Partners), incorporating a cinema. The office floors are designed for easy sub-division for letting, and each floor is separately air-conditioned. Construction is reinforced concrete, with dark green marble facing on the ground floor and white bush-hammered plaster above. The fins are faced with yellow glass mosaic and the windows on the main (west) façade have asbestos louvres. On the north and south façades they are angled to give protection from the sun. The steel windows are locally made.

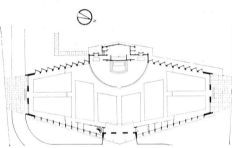

plan of Catholic church

Above: Roman Catholic church (architect, Alfred Wong), dedicated to St Bernadette. It seats 1,200 and has reinforced concrete columns and steel beams, exposed internally, supporting a light steel deck roof. There is a choir balcony over the main entrance. Bells are housed in the small tower below the flèche.

Victoria Theatre (architects, James Cubitt, Leonard Manasseh and Partners): the internal reconstruction of a theatre of 1896 within the original walls. The air-conditioned main auditorium has 950 seats and is designed for use as a theatre, cinema and concert-hall and for public meetings. There are also a rehearsal theatre seating 150, a large foyer, four bars and dressing-rooms for 75.

Government adult education centre (architect, M. J. Cotton, Public Works Department). It has an air-conditioned theatre for 350 people, with a full stage, at the upper level. Below this are study-rooms, offices and a bar. Construction is reinforced concrete.

Below: St. Anthony's Friary (architect, Alfred Wong), for the Franciscan Fathers. The site is about fifteen miles from Singapore city with wide views of the countryside. The main building (on left of photograph) has the refectory, workroom and reception-rooms on the ground floor and fourteen bedrooms above. It is connected by a covered way to the chapel (right in photograph), which has roofs at two levels, forming a clerestory that admits light to the altar. Construction is reinforced concrete with tiled timber roofs.

Right: St Peter's Hall, a residential college for Anglican students (architects, E. E. Keen and Partners). Accommodation includes chapel, refectory, library, common-room, three small flats for married students, and fifteen rooms for single students. The site slopes steeply, but a level platform was left by the demolition of an earlier building. This produced an east-west orientation for the main frontages; hence the angled windows to protect rooms from the morning and afternoon sun. Construction is reinforced concrete with brick infill walls and a timber roof.

House at Belmont (architects, James W. Ferrier and Partners), on a suburban site. The main interest is on the garden side (shown here). The living and dining rooms on a lower level are connected with the bedroom wing, which overlooks a private courtyard, by a bridge across a pool.

Senior officers' quarters, Kay Siang Road (architect, Lincoln Page, Singapore Improvement Trust): planned with changing levels, determined by the slope of the site. The lowest level has the garage, main entrance, stores and servants' rooms. Steps from this level lead to a central lounge that separates feeding from living areas, and a few more steps lead to the bedroom and bathroom wing which runs at right angles to the lower part of the building (on the right in the photograph). Load-bearing walls are of hollow blocks.

Brunei and North Borneo

THESE TERRITORIES have an ancient history of trading in spices, camphor and gold, of conquest by Malay sultans, of piracy and general adventure ranging from visits by Chinese merchants in the sixth century through the visit of Magellan in the early sixteenth century and right up to Joseph Conrad, the Rajahs Brooke and the early rule of the Chartered Company. The indigenous people are Muruts, Dyaks, Kelabits and others who are still in a fairly underdeveloped state, and who live in the jungles or in fishing-villages by the sea. Malays conquered them and ruled them from very early times, but established themselves only in town and villages along the coast or by rivers. British rule commenced in North Borneo by the Chartered Company about 1870. Brunei, which formerly ruled all over this group, has shrunk to the smallest but has always been ruled by a Sultan, of late under British guidance. It has recently been granted a new constitution and is rapidly moving towards complete self-government.

British North Borneo is a quiet, pleasant place, which is developing slowly on a good stable basis. Towns are growing, industry and agriculture are being developed and there is every reason for the inhabitants to look to a steady and fairly prosperous future. Most of the towns were razed by one side or the other in the last war but have since been rebuilt to unexciting but sensible straightforward plans. The State of Brunei has a totally different post-war history. It too was devastated during the war, but the enormous increase in the production of oil by the Brunei Shell Petroleum Company has led to a very rapid rebuilding of the towns. There has unfortunately been no town-plan, and a great opportunity was lost when a whole town sprang up with many good modern buildings, both private and government, which had little relationship to each other. Large parts of the original river town, consisting of wooden and thatched buildings on stilts, remain however. Many such surround the new mosque, which was one of the first post-war buildings to be started, built to a basically traditional design as required by the Sultan. It provides a focal point in the town (which is built on flat land), a focal point soon to be reinforced by the proposed new Lapau and Dewan Majlis or Houses of Parliament, which are a modern development of a traditional design. The Shell Company have not only assisted enormously in the development of these countries by their oil production, but have created a completely new town at Seria in Brunei, where the main oil fields are.

Owing to the large areas of flat, swampy land by the coast, many buildings have to be piled. Local contractors now have a high degree of skill in piling. They are also skilled in reinforced concrete work, but are poor in brickwork, plastering and finishes generally, although Chinese masons are excellent at tiling. Building is made more difficult by having to use salt beach sand, since there is little inland or river sand owing to the geological nature of the countries. The only technical school for artisans is run by the Shell Company, so there are few skilled artisans among the local population. Most of the carpenters, bricklayers, steel workers and so on are Chinese, and are brought in on contract for particular projects from Singapore or Hong Kong.

The problems of building in this climate are now well known. Heat and humidity are the main things to overcome and, if it is to be done by natural means, this involves basic one-room-deep buildings with the maximum cross ventilation and the use of ceiling fans. This then raises the problem of wind control, so some form of adjustable louvre is generally used in windows. The advantages of complete air-conditioning of buildings are now being recognized and many new projects are being so treated. The additional expense is, of course, generally not great since the cube of the buildings can be reduced. Roofs, pitched or flat, must be insulated and sun and rain must be kept from walls and windows. This is achieved traditionally by overhanging eaves or open verandahs, but a variety of adjustable or fixed brise-soleils, screen walls and so on are now also used.

PETER MORLEY

Brunei

Government offices, etc., Kuala Belait (architects, Booty, Edwards and Partners), which includes an office block, a post-office and a court-house. Right: the east side of the office block with the octagonal post-office in the background. The structure, including piling, is reinforced concrete. Windows, doors and sun-breakers are of anodized aluminium because of the corrosive salt atmosphere.

A detail from the same group of government buildings: the entry, across a pool, to the court-house which lies to the west of the office block.

**ground floor plan,
officers' quarters**

key
1, bedrooms.
2, living area.
3, dining area.
4, kitchen.
5, garage.
6, servants.
7, laundry.

Senior Government officers' quarters (architects,
Public Works Department, Brunei): a group of
identical single-storey houses, each with living-rooms
and bedrooms separated by a courtyard (see plan
of individual house on left). The two wings of each
house are linked by a trellis. They have load-bearing
cavity end walls. The side walls, facing both inwards
and outwards, are all window or louvred panels.

Broadcasting studios, Kuala Belait (architects, James Cubitt, Leonard
Manasseh and Partners). It contains studios, a library, offices, control-
rooms and waiting-space, all air-conditioned and planned round small
garden courts. Construction is reinforced concrete. The building is raised
in the centre to give clerestory lighting and ventilation.

Above: flats at Tasek (architects, Booty, Edwards and Partners): a rectangular block placed across the contours of a sloping site, which thus gives six storeys at one end and four at the other. The building contains 50 flats altogether, each with a living-room facing south and two bedrooms facing north. The photograph shows the south side with projecting staircase-towers and access balconies.

Flats in Brunei town (architects, Booty, Edwards and Partners): a three-storey block with covered balconies the full width of each living-room. Access is by a semi-open staircase at the end of the block. Construction is reinforced concrete.

Girls' school, Brunei town (architects, Booty Edwards and Partners): a two-storey building planned round an open court, with sun-screening either by means of vertical fins (right of photograph) or decorative concrete grilles (on the left). Construction is reinforced concrete with brick infill panels and timber roofs. The roofs are covered with glazed tiles.

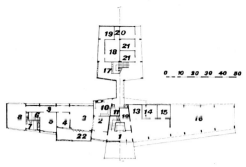

half upper floor (left) and ground floor (right) of flats at Jesselton

key: 1, lift lobby. 2, dining room. 3, living room. 4, study. 5, 8, bedrooms. 6, 7, bathrooms. 9, passage. 10, kitchen. 11, 12, 13, 14, 15, stores. 16, garage. 17, ironing. 18, servant. 19, servant's kitchen. 20, lavatory. 21, store. 22, terrace.

Flats at Signal Hill, Jesselton (architects, Palmer and Turner): twelve two- or three-bedroom flats with servants' quarters additional, planned in two linked blocks at right-angles (see plan above). Construction is reinforced concrete with brick infill panels.

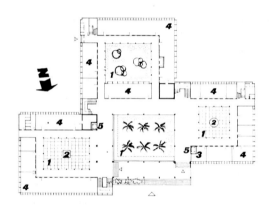

ground floor plan, central government offices at Jesselton

key: 1, terraces, 2, fountains. 3, enquiry office. 4, offices. 5, lifts.

Central Government offices, Jesselton (architect, R. Gordon Brown). Three blocks, each planned round a courtyard, form three sides of a tree-planted square (see plan above). Construction is reinforced concrete on a 2-ft. 8-in. grid, on concrete piling. Sun-control is by galvanized steel or slatted timber louvres and an air-space between the double reinforced concrete roof.

Hong Kong

IN 1841 THIS BARREN ISLAND ROCK was ceded to the British with a population of about 4,000 villagers and fishermen, living in some 50 villages or hamlets. In 1860 the colony was extended on to the Kowloon Peninsula, and in 1898 the British again extended, acquiring under a 99-year lease a substantial piece of the mainland near Kowloon and a group of islands, now together known as the New Territories. Urban development has been concentrated largely in Victoria, on Hong Kong Island itself, though since the war Kowloon – across the harbour from the island – has also grown enormously.

The area available on Hong Kong Island for urban building was originally no more than a narrow strip of comparatively level ground along the foreshore. As the nineteenth century proceeded, the tiers of houses gradually rose up the sides of the rock, the fashionable residential area rising at the same time. Reclamation of land from the sea began in the Colony's earliest days, and continued in spite of much opposition from the principal commercial houses with foreshore sites. It failed, however, to keep apace with the increasing population. In 1870 the central part of Victoria, chiefly by now occupied by Chinese, was seriously overcrowded and insanitary. This was one of the factors that led the European community to climb even higher and develop the summits of the Peak as a residential area, a movement hastened from 1888 onwards when Peak and city were linked by a funicular railway. The Colony continued thereafter to grow steadily, but its most spectacular increase in population took place after the end of the second World War.

A brief period of military administration was followed by the formal re-establishment of civil government in May, 1946. From the moment of liberation from the Japanese, Hong Kong made an astonishing recovery. In August, 1945, it was estimated that the population had been reduced to about 600,000. Eighteen months later at least 1,000,000 people had returned, and the population was still rising. Once again there was an acute housing problem and water shortage. At the end of 1959 the population was estimated at 2,919,000.

One of the most striking features of the post-war years has been the steadily increasing part which the Government has begun to play, directly or indirectly, in the provision of housing and other forms of social services for this increasing population, and especially for the poorer sections of the community. But in addition private building on a wide scale has transformed and modernized much of the urban areas and the more accessible parts of the New Territories.

Particularly in Kowloon and Tsuen Wan, industrialists have opened large modern factories, producing a wide range of goods for export throughout the world. To meet the demand for more land for industry and housing, the Government has continued the traditional policy of reclamation. It has also embarked on a large-scale reconstruction of the Colony's road network. More rigorous traffic controls have been introduced in the face of enlarged public transport services and the increase in number, and in size, of private cars in daily use. The railway has changed from steam to diesel-electric traction.

The Government, with an unusually progressive and well staffed Public Works Department, has also been active in the provision of schools and hospitals. One of Hong Kong's major problems, at a time of continual refugee influx, has been the provision of adequate medical and health facilities, both official and unofficial. The Colony's earliest hospitals were run by missionary bodies, as indeed are a number at the present time. The first Government hospital was the Civil Hospital, founded in 1859. Part of its large old-fashioned buildings is still in use, and on the remainder of the original site there stands today the spacious and modern Tsan Yuk Maternity Hospital, opened in 1925, and the Queen Mary Hospital, one of the largest and most up to date in Asia, opened in 1937. This is now being doubled in size.

An increased and ever increasing tempo is apparent in every aspect of Hong Kong's daily life, but it is the growth of local industry, which came into being to replace the traditional entrepôt trade of the Colony, that has been the most significant feature, after population growth, of the post-war years.

In 1955 two changes in the law allowed much higher building, and made it very much easier to get possession of tenanted buildings by compensating the evicted tenants. As a result, buildings between fourteen and twenty storeys high are becoming common, particularly in Victoria and in the newly built area to the east, from Causeway Bay to North Point, in a burst of building in which Hong Kong is trying to catch up with the demand for housing. The old solution of making land by reclamation or levelling is still in vigorous progress; but instead of the new land being covered with closely packed buildings, there are tall square blocks with plenty of breathing space between. In the town centres, particularly in Victoria, buildings sometimes in excellent repair are being torn down to be replaced by much higher ones. Gradually the pre-war arcaded building, with square pillars covered in Chinese characters denoting the names of the shops, is giving way to the steel-framed structures whose overhanging, if any, needs no pillars and leaves the pavement clear.

The provision of housing, probably the most important field of enterprise in Hong Kong at the present time, is faced by planning problems quite different from those of the West, if only because of the shortage of land on which to build and the extremes of accommodation demanded. These range from flats with space-standards as low as 35 square feet per person, plus kitchen and lavatory, to flats and houses of Western standard, from 800 to as much as 3,000 square feet in area, but with quarters for living-in servants. The servants' rooms are generally next to the kitchen and must not be seen from the main rooms. Chinese cooking, which involves a lot of deep-fat frying, together with the high cost and expensive upkeep of mechanical ventilation, makes internal kitchens and bathrooms undesirable. As a result the average plan of a block of flats has a large perimeter, with all such rooms provided with windows on an outside wall.

Speculative building is organized on the basis of a quick return of the capital invested (between three and five years), which limits the architect's scope in the way of refinements in details and demands the use of lasting materials. Such speedy designing and building tend to result in buildings which are cliché-ridden. Novel features introduced into any building are repeated in others *ad nauseam*. Such repetition in itself is partially, however, responsible for a place producing its own style – or a style with its own peculiar clichés – and Hong Kong's contacts with the outside world are so close, conditions for import are so liberal, that anything which is economically viable is adopted and adapted.

Hong Kong is about 20 degrees north of the Equator and has a hot, humid summer and a dry winter period of several months, during which the temperature never falls to freezing but cold winds and clouded skies make heating in buildings necessary. It is in the typhoon area, and winds of 134 miles per hour have been recorded. The building industry is highly skilled and local materials are good though limited to sand and stone.

Excellent well-seasoned teak is available and is much used for flooring, outdoor woodwork and furniture. The Chinese carpenter uses primitive tools but is a sensitive and competent craftsman. Locally manufactured bricks and tiles now replace those formerly imported from China, but their range is limited. There are also local ceramic units, which are widely used for grilles and the like.

In the pre-war days, most of the practising architects either came from abroad or had set up on their own after serving as articled pupils under the same architects. Since the second World War the refugees from mainland China who have flooded into Hong Kong have included a great number of architects and architectural assistants. These, like the earlier established architects, are for the most part men trained in Europe or the United States, so the heritage of native Chinese architecture has little influence on present-day building, except for some motives derived from it, employed in such details as decorative grilles.

Even the Chinese architects had for the most part a Western training, until in 1950 an architectural school was started by the University of Hong Kong. The first group of students completed their course in 1955. Most of the graduates are now working with the local architects but a few have established their own practices.

ERIC CUMINE

Low-cost housing at Sai Wan Chuen (West Bay Village), for the Hong Kong Housing Authority (architect, T. S. C. Feltham). It consists of five blocks of one-room-deep flats (to provide cross-ventilation) placed across the contours of a hillside site. The approach road enters the scheme at the half-way level, from which there are lifts to all floors above but stairs only to the floors below. There are 640 flats, varying in size for four-, five- and six-person families. Both balcony and staircase access are used.

Police married quarters, Arsenal Yard (architects, Public Works Department; architect in charge, T. T. Wong). A primary school occupies the whole ground floor. Above are ten floors of thirty dwellings, each consisting of one large all-purpose room with a verandah facing south, the kitchen forming part of the verandah. Access is from balconies along the north side, reached by lifts. Lavatories and washrooms are grouped in two separate projecting wings, with a drying-space between. Construction is reinforced concrete bearing walls.

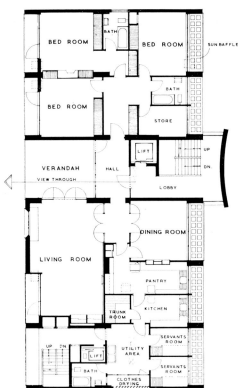

Staff quarters for the Hong Kong Electric Co., called Cavendish Heights (architects, Leigh and Orange). The blocks are linked by a courtyard and contain identical flats, one to each floor. They face north-west and south-east with views over the harbour. Since many of the occupants are engineers engaged on shift-work, the flats (see plan) have been divided into noisy and quiet areas separated by the lift, staircase, entrance and main verandah. The quiet area, containing three bedrooms and two bathrooms, can be separately air-conditioned. The living-room and dining-room can be thrown into one. There is covered drying-space on the roof of each block.

plan: Cavendish Heights

Low-cost housing at So Uk (architects, the Hong Kong Housing Authority). Part of a high-density estate on a steeply sloping site, comprising 5,302 flats in 8-storey, 12-storey and 16-storey blocks and housing a population of 33,000. The site covers 18½ acres and, besides the housing, has two primary schools, a community hall, 38 shops and a sports ground.

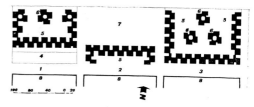

site plan: housing at North Point

key: 1, west estate. **2**, centre estate. **3**, east estate. **4**, government printing works. **5**, playgrounds. **6**, point blocks. **7**, bus concourse. **8**, existing buildings.

Below: low-cost housing, North Point (architect, Eric Cumine), for the Hong Kong Housing Authority, accommodating 12,300 people (see plan) and giving a density of 2,000 per acre. There are wide promenades along the harbour frontage. The tower blocks in the middle of the two flanking sections have covered play-areas at ground level and ten floors of flats above. The scheme includes a community centre and 71 shops. Later there will be a bus terminus and a ferry pier. The flats vary in size to house from three to eight people. Construction is reinforced concrete with brick infill walls.

Flats – Tower Court – (architect, Eric Cumine): a block
facing north and south containing a variety of flats from
single-room studio flats to maisonettes that occupy
almost two complete floors. All living and bedrooms
have balconies and all bedrooms connected bathrooms.
The maisonettes are entered at the bedroom level with
the living-rooms above, in order to allow kitchens, etc.,
to face the back without interfering with horizontal
circulation, and to restrict noise-transmission from
living-rooms to the bedrooms of the same flat. The whole
eleventh floor is occupied as offices by the Indian
Consulate together with a two-bedroom flat. The
twelfth floor is one large flat. Half the thirteenth and
the whole of the fourteenth floor together form a large
penthouse maisonette with five bedrooms and living-
room and dining-room which, when united by sliding
doors, occupy half the floor-area of the building. The
other half of the thirteenth floor is a full-width one-room
flat.

Staff flats, Hong Kong University (architect, R. Gordon Brown; assistant architect, Lars Myrenberg). They stand on a steep site in the University grounds, facing west over the harbour. The saw-tooth plan turns the windows away from the sun. There are three flats per floor, two with two bedrooms and one with one bedroom. The flats are constructed on a reinforced concrete frame with cross-walls of local granite; the detail on the facing page shows the contrast in texture between the granite and the smooth concrete surfaces. Louvres and other external woodwork are of teak.

key
1, lobby.
2, living and dining rooms.
3, verandah.
4, bedroom.
5, bathroom.
6, kitchen.
7, servant.
8, balcony.
9, lift and stairs.

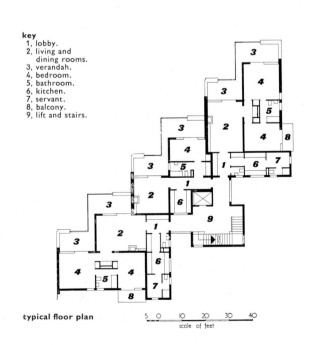

typical floor plan

scale of feet

One of the balconies of the flats shown on the facing page, with view over the harbour.

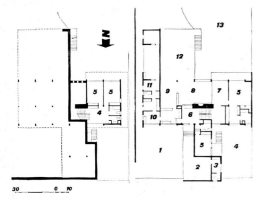

30   0 10

lower ground floor   **ground floor**

key
1, yard.
2, garage.
3, chauffeur.
4, children's playing areas.
5, bedrooms.
6, foyer.
7, study.
8, living room
9, dining room.
10, kitchen.
11, servants.
12, terrace.
13, garden.

House on a hillside across the harbour from
Hong Kong Island (architect, Stanley T. Kwok).
It is on two levels (see plan). All main rooms face
south and get the benefit of the view and prevailing
sea-breezes. The apparent size of the living-room
is increased by a study-ante-room to the main
bedroom in the form of a balcony. Beneath are
children's bedrooms adjoining a play area and two
more bathrooms. The house has a reinforced
concrete frame.

Below: the entrance (south) elevation of the building
housing the Department of Chemistry, Hong Kong
University (architect, R. Gordon Brown; assistant
architect, Lars Myrenberg). It contains teaching
and research laboratories, two lecture halls and
storage accommodation. The building is of
reinforced concrete frame construction, plastered
externally and finished in strong colours. Between
the concrete vertical members of the entrance front
are grey-coloured panels of Shanghai plaster.

Chapel at Wah Yan College, for the Jesuit Order, on Mount Parish (architect, R. Gordon Brown). Above: the chapel seen across the college courtyard. On the right is a classroom wing and, beyond, a covered playground with laboratories above. Right: the interior; wall panels are of local brick.

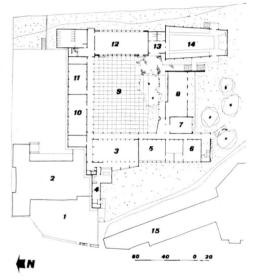

ground floor: training college, Kowloon

key: 1, car park. 2, existing assembly hall. 3, dining room. 4, kitchen. 5, handicraft room. 6, pottery room. 7, project room. 8, study room. 9, paved area. 10, female students. 11, male students. 12, existing gymnasium. 13, foyer. 14 lecture hall.

Teachers' training college, Kowloon (architects, Public Works Department; architect in charge, D. G. Farrow): an extension of the original Grantham training college. The new accommodation (see plan) consists of lecture and tutorial rooms and special classrooms, library, refectory and a lecture-hall seating 340 also used for practice instruction of primary school children. Access balconies, projecting eaves, vertical fins and pre-cast concrete grilles protect the rooms from the sun. Construction is reinforced concrete with a steel truss roof over the lecture hall. Infill walls are rendered brick.

Right: office building (architects, Leigh and Orange) known as Caxton House. The façade treatment derives from the need to enable individual tenants to install their own air-conditioning, the units for which can be fitted behind the louvred panels beneath the windows, avoiding the unsightly exposure of air-conditioning units which often occurs when there is no central plant.

Above: Central Government offices (architects, Public Works Department; architects in charge, J. C. Charter, J. T. Mallorie, A. Fitch and J. B. Aitken). The building is T-shaped (see plans), with a council chamber at the end of one wing, and is sited above the centre of Victoria city. The height was kept low so as not to obstruct views over the harbour from Government House, further up the hill. The air-conditioned offices are 19 ft. deep and planned on a 4-ft. 6-in. window bay. The fins between windows are part of the structural concrete frame. Below the windows are slate panels separated by pre-cast mullions.

Below (right): Government primary school, Kowloon (architect, W. Szeto). It has 24 classrooms, each for 45 pupils, three larger specialized teaching rooms, offices, staff rooms, etc. At ground-floor level (see plan below), a covered playground links the staircase hall with the single-storey lavatory block and the classrooms over. These are given north-lighting by a saw-tooth plan. The entrance block contains the special teaching and staff rooms, also over a covered playground.

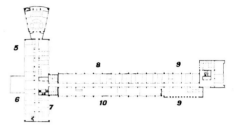

first floor

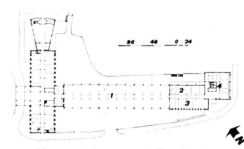

ground floor: central government offices: key: 1, car park. **2**, paying office. **3**, dining room. **4**, clinic. **5**, council chamber suite. **6**, quartering authority. **7**, legal department. **8, 10**, building ordinance offices. **9**, port works offices.

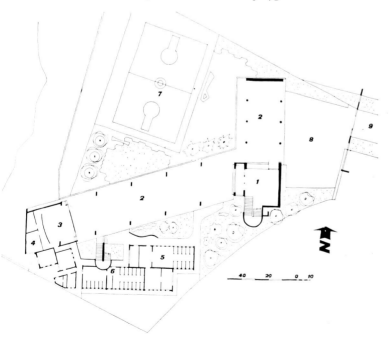

ground floor: school at Kowloon

key: 1, entrance hall. **2**, covered playground. **3**, platform. **4**, dressing room. **5**, boys' lavatory. **6**, girls' lavatory. **7**, basket ball court. **8**, car park. **9**, approach road.

Ferry concourse and car-park, Hong Kong (architects, Public Works Department; architects-in-charge, A. Fitch and R. J. Phillips). The ferry is the main link between the island of Hong Kong and Kowloon, on the north side of the harbour. The three-tier car-park, with which has been combined paved pedestrian areas and covered waiting spaces to serve the crowds using the ferry, is built on land reclaimed from the harbour near the centre of the city. Above: the reinforced concrete car-park (which accommodates 405 cars) showing the structurally independent ramp, on the east side and the open grille which screens the centre storey. Below: the opposite (west) side, with a 16-ft. cantilevered concrete canopy beneath which ferry passengers can alight from their cars.

UNDERLINED ON MAPS of the Commonwealth are many island territories too small to be coloured in red: places like St Helena, once important as a port of call on the route to India; Bermuda, now a luxury resort off the US Eastern Seaboard; and Mauritius, Indian Ocean sugar island whose people – though mostly Hindu – speak French. The largest number of these islands lie in the Caribbean Sea and the Pacific Ocean. The West Indies are well known; their architecture is described and illustrated elsewhere in this volume.

We know less about the Pacific Islands. Before the Japanese War the names which came first to mind would have been Tahiti, a French island, and Hawaii, which recently became the 49th of the United States. Japanese invasion and American reconquest gave fame to such names as Guadalcanal in the British Solomon Islands and Tarawa, one of the Gilbert and Ellis Islands. The personality of Queen Salote interested Coronation Londoners in Tonga, another small Pacific island.

Most important of these islands is the Fiji Group, which straddles the 180 degree meridian and lies about 1,200 miles south of the equator on the air route from Hawaii to Australia. It includes 300 islands, about 100 of which are inhabited; but only two are of any importance, Viti Levu and Vanua Levu. It is on the first, Viti Levu, where are to be found the islands' capital, Suva, its international airport, Nandi, and two of its main sources of wealth – sugar and gold. Its other main source of wealth – the growing of coconuts for copra, a romantically lazy but not very profitable pastime – is distributed throughout the group.

First mapped by William Bligh of *Bounty* fame, the islands were mainly inhabited by a predominantly Melanesian people when, in 1874, under a Deed of Cession, they were handed over by the Fijian Chiefs to Queen Victoria as a Protectorate. Though now second in number to immigrant peoples of Indian descent, the Fijians still enjoy special rights, particularly on land matters. The total population of the group is about 370,000.

An engraving of the 1874 cession ceremonies shows a verandahed range of corrugated iron roofed offices where the new Administration had established its headquarters. They contrast sadly with the Fijians' own traditional thatched 'bures'. Unfortunately, as in many other countries, the materials needed for traditional rural building techniques – like reeds and bamboos, which grow wild – are becoming scarce as more land comes under cultivation. Skills are dying out, and the 'bures' are being replaced by timber and sheeted cottages.

Until recently, much of the building in Fiji was in wood, usually with corrugated iron or asbestos cement sheet roofs. Many of the architects and builders came from New Zealand or Australia and brought techniques and styles with them. In recent years, concrete has become a popular material. Cement and most other building materials have to be imported. The only local material of any importance is timber, likely to be used increasingly as modern preservative techniques are introduced. (Fiji suffers seriously from dry wood termite infestation.)

Lying 18 degrees south, Fiji enjoys a tropical island climate tempered by cool breezes in the winter season (May to October). Suva, the capital, is on the wetter side of Viti Levu. Its climate, being more humid, less sunny and with more breezeless days, is less pleasant than that at Nandi, on the north-west coast. Like other islands lying towards the tropics, Fiji from time to time is struck by hurricanes, the last serious storm being in 1952.

G. A. ATKINSON

Fiji

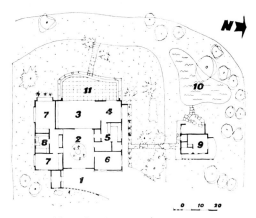

ground floor plan, house at Tamavua

key
1, garage.
2, courtyard.
3, living room.
4, dining room.
5, kitchen.
6, study-bedroom.
7, bedrooms.
8, bathroom.
9, servants.
10, pool.
11, terrace.

House at Tamavua seen from the north-west (architect, Hans Furrer). It was built for the architect's own occupation. The site is high up, with a wide view over the nearby hills and over Suva harbour, and is orientated to face the view and make the best use of the prevailing breeze. The rooms are grouped round a central yard (see plan) which is roofed with glass. The house has a reinforced concrete frame with concrete block panel-walls reinforced horizontally against earthquakes and hurricanes. Roofs are constructed of timber which has been treated against termites, and are covered with galvanized corrugated iron. The main bedroom has movable vertical sun-screens (seen on the far right in the illustration) and the living-room verandah has horizontal louvres.

Central medical school seen from the north-east (C. N. Nettleton, Government architect). It contains hostel and teaching accommodation for 100 students. The U-shaped plan has a central wing containing the assembly-hall. Access is from open balconies.

Shopping arcade at Suva, with offices over (architect, Gordon J. Larsen). It is planned round three sides of a paved square, open to the south-east which is the direction of the prevailing breeze (see plan on left). The offices are reached from a balcony that overhangs the entrances to the shops.

ground floor: shopping arcade at Suva

key
1, service courts.
2, shops.
3, stores.
4, access ways.
5, centre court.

Offices and shops, Suva (architects, Larsen and Associates). Built across a sloping site, it has shops on the ground floor with two floors of office space above. At the lower end (left of illustration) is a free-standing stair-tower, elliptical in shape.

Photographic Acknowledgments

Page 4 (frontispiece) photograph by Roy Tsang, reproduced by courtesy of the Otis Elevator Co.

AUSTRALIA. Pages 20 (right), 28, Wolfgang Stevers. Page 21 (top), Douglass Baglin. Page 21 (bottom), D. Darian Smith. Pages 22, 23 (bottom), 30, 31 (top), 33 (top), 38, 40 (bottom), 41, Max Dupain and Kerry Dundas. Pages 24 (top), 33 (bottom left), Australian News and Information Bureau. Page 25 (bottom), Risko and Kos. Page 26, Herald Sun Photograph. Page 27 (top), Corke and Clabburn. Page 27 (bottom), Ronald H. Armstrong. Page 29 (top), L. and D. Keen (Brisbane). Page 29 (bottom), Brisbane City Council Department of Works. Page 31 (bottom), Colorcraft Photography Pty. Pages 36, 37, Marc Strizic. Page 39, Associated General Publications. Page 40 (top), Gordon F. De'Lisle.

NEW ZEALAND: Pages 46, 51 (top), Sparrow Industrial Pictures. Page 47 (top and centre), R. A. Ayton. Page 47 (bottom), R. V. Francis Smith. Page 48 (bottom left), G. H. Burt. Page 51 (bottom), Barry McKay. Pages 52, 53, M. D. King. Pages 54 (top), 57 (top left and top right), 58, 59, Martin Barriball. Page 60 (bottom), Hi-Light Studios. Page 61, Bruce Watt Studio. Pages 62 (top), 63, 64, Mannering and Donaldson. Page 62 (bottom), George Wetzel.

CANADA: Page 69, Thompson, Berwick and Pratt. Page 70 (top), Arnott and Rogers. Pages 70 (bottom and right), 80 (top and bottom), 81, 82 (bottom), 83 (top), 86 (top left and bottom), 87 (bottom), 88, 89, 91, 92 (top), Max Fleet. Pages 71, 73, 74, 75, 79, 80 (centre), 84 (top and centre), 85 (bottom), 86 (top right), 92 (bottom), 93, Panda. Pages 72 (bottom), 84 (bottom), Wells Studio. Page 76 (top), Brian Shawcroft. Page 76 (bottom), Alberta Government Photograph. Pages 77, 83 (bottom), Svarre Cantlon. Page 78 (top and centre), Ben Schnall. Page 82 (top), Studio Alain Enrg. Page 85 (top), Belair. Page 87 (top), E. W. Cadman. Page 90 (top), G. Milne and Co. Page 90 (bottom), J. Parkin. Page 94 (centre and bottom), Leonard Frank Photographers.

WEST AFRICA: Pages 107, 108, D. A. Barratt. Pages 109 (bottom), 111 (bottom), 112, I. J. Rose-Innes. Pages 113–17, Peter Pitt. Page 118, Harry Weese and Associates. Page 119, Ministry of Works (Crown copyright). Page 123 (second from bottom), R. Lannoy. Page 124 (bottom), David Dupree.

EAST AFRICA: Pages 134, 135, 136 (bottom), 137 (top), J. H. Beers. Page 136 (top), Peter Heathcote. Page 137 (centre), East African Railways and Harbours. Page 137 (bottom), Standard Pic. Pages 138 (top), 142 (top), R. Ward. Pages 139 (bottom), 141 (top), Department of Information, Uganda Government. Pages 143, 144 (top and centre), Public Relations Department, Tanganyika. Page 144 (bottom), Studio Paramount.

THE RHODESIAS: Page 149 (top), Rho-Scott. Page 153, *Architecture and Design*. Page 154 (bottom), 155, John Akester. Page 156 (top), Robal Studio. Page 158 (bottom), Federal Power Board. Pages 159 (top), 160, Sylvia Beck (PVT) Ltd. Page 159 (bottom) Camera Craft.

THE CARIBBEAN: Pages 165, 166, 167 (top and right), 168 (two top), 169, A. D. Porter. Page 167 (second from top), Paul O. Rupp. Page 168 (two bottom), Chan's Photographers. Page 170, Tom Leonard. Page 171, Noel Norton. Page 172, Tell Precision Co. Ltd. Pages 173 (bottom), 175, 176 (centre and bottom), Gerry Murison. Page 174, Gick. Page 177 (bottom right), Skerritt. Pages 178 (bottom), 179 (top), L. St Helene. Pages 179 (bottom), 180 (bottom), Fitzpatrick Studios.

INDIA, PAKISTAN AND CEYLON: Pages 184 (bottom), 185, 186, 187 (bottom right), 188 (top), Valerie Winter. Page 189 (bottom), Ramzan K. Mundrawala. MALAYA: Pages 197, 198 (top), Ng. Bros. Studios. Page 199 (top), Federal Information Department. Page 199 (bottom), Mellow Yap Photo Co. Pages 200, 202 (top), Lee and Sons.

SINGAPORE: Pages 206 (top), 208 (top), 209 (bottom), 210 (top), Tong Photo Service. Pages 206 (bottom), 207 (two top), 210 (bottom), Singapore Improvement Trust. Page 208 (bottom), M. Bile Foto Service. Page 209 (top), M. J. Cotton. Page 210 (centre), L. J. W. Goring. NORTH BORNEO: Page 216, Gordon Wells. HONG KONG: Page 221 (top), T. T. Wong and Public Works Department, Hong Kong. Page 230, Public Works Department, Hong Kong.

FIJI: Page 233 (top), Stinsons. Page 234 (top), Art Studio, Suva.

236

Index